**The Magic Circle
Forming and Running a Wiccan Coven**

Disclaimer

This work is the copyright of the author and may not be reproduced in any form.

The publisher and author have sought to verify the information in this text but do not take responsibility for errors or omissions or for alternative interpretations.

This book is provided for informational purposes only and is not intended to diagnose or treat any condition. Please consult with your doctor or healthcare provider in regards to any medical issue.

Keeping to the laws of any national or state jurisdiction is the responsibility of the reader. Nothing in this text should be taken to encourage breaking of any law, or to encourage cruelty to animals.

The publisher and author provide these contents on an 'as is' basis and make no representation or warranties in regards to its contents.

The author and publisher do not assume liability to anyone purchasing or reading this text.

All attempts have been made to avoid any slight to any individual or organisation and no intentional offence is contained in this text.

Published by Cochrane Faithful
21 Princes Road Ealing
Copyright © 2020 by Cochrane Faithful

A beginning is a very delicate time

Princess Irulan
Dune (1984)

Contents

Introduction
1. What is a coven ?
2. Why do covens do ?
3. Why form a coven
4. Connecting with the Wiccan Community
5. Finding a lineage
6. Creating a grimoire and assembling tools
7. Creating a training course
8. Committing to starting a coven
9. Getting connected and preparing to form a coven
10. Finding a magical site and running the first rite
11. Forming a pre-coven
12. Bringing people into an existing pre-coven
13. Events for a pre-coven
14. Building the coven's structure
15. Formally initiating the coven
16. The first year of running a coven
17. Dealing with problems
18. Keeping a coven running after one year
Conclusion

Intro

Wicca is the modern incarnation of the Old Religion of Britain. That spiritual practice was termed Witchcraft, and was illegal in Britain before 1951. Following the repeal of the Witchcraft Act a number of traditions appeared. In 1964 many of the representatives of these traditions gathered in London where they were addressed by Doreen Valiente. Valiante is a prominent witch of the modern era and at that time was a member of the Thames Valley Coven of Robert Cochrane, the foremost Traditional Witch of the modern era. At this dinner Valiente promoted the Wiccan Rede, 'an it harm none do what ye will'.

Over time many groups defined themselves as Wiccans basing their practice on the Wiccan Rede. Most practice solitary, however some joined together and formed groups of witches, termed covens. One of the most prominent books about Wicca 'Wicca for the Solitary Practitioner' by Scott Cunningham provides a detailed explanation about how a Wiccan can practice solitary. For some, however, working in a group is part of being a Wiccan, and many are not satisfied by solitary practice.

The problem faced by those who want to practice in a coven is that it is often very difficult to find one to work with. If a coven can be found then the individual is likely to take up that option, however many coven members have to travel long distances to their coven and ultimately may wish to set up their own. Additionally covens disband and a Wiccan who has been a member of a coven is likely to want to join another, which may be impossible if there are none accepting members.

For many Wiccans there will be a time when they want to form their own coven. This can be challenging since there are many issues to be faced. How will members be found ? Where will the coven meet ? What rituals will be performed and which grimoire will be used ? These issues can be a challenge, even for those with a long history of coven membership and may appear to be overwhelming for the novice. For those who are determined, however, these obstacles can be overcome. The efforts are invariably repaid and many who have been members of covens will attest to the benefits of working with a group of Wiccans.

1. What is a Coven ?

There are many ways that people view covens. They are often seen as groups of friends, and this is generally what they become. When covens start, however, those that survive generally begin as a group of students around a teacher, and those that don't begin in this way often ultimately fail. Building a strong coven is not simply a case of strong ritual practice. Ultimately teaching is often required.

Recognising the central role of teaching helps to explain how a coven develops. The development is driven by the fact that at the centre is someone who really understands what Wicca is and how it can help the individual. For this reason to start a coven requires the individual who is creating it to have a good understanding of Wicca, and also magic, and how it works in practice. They need to explain how the practice works and how it can benefit the individual.

This means that until the coven is established it often takes a great deal of work and requires the person running it to have direct contact with a large number of people until the coven is formed. Its formation is not a straightforward task because disagreements occur and this can break up the group.

A coven is universally understood to be a group of witches. Many see coven based Witchcraft as a form of practice that existed in the past, however covens continue to exist in the modern era. Their form is closely related to that in the historical record, however since the legalisation of Witchcraft in 1951 the former practice has become more open and covens have developed. Nonetheless the historically understood form of thirteen practitioners of the old craft working under the leadership of a Maiden and a Magister, with the support of a Summoner, remains a widespread form of Witchcraft practice in the modern era.

Covens are ultimately a form of spiritual practice that takes place according to the lunar and solar cycles. But covens are also groups of friends who gather together and in addition to rituals socialise and support each other in other ways.

Nonetheless at the heart of any Wiccan Coven practice is the monthly forming of a magic circle at the full moon at which magic is practised. These covens do not practice in isolation and are connected with other covens both historically and also in the modern era.

Within Wicca there are two fundamental forms of practice and almost all covens are derived from one or other of these. These practices relate to the development of Witchcraft in the period immediately following the repeal of the witchcraft act in 1951. Following this a witchcraft museum was established by Cecil Williamson in the Isle of Man. He was himself not a witch however he worked with Gerald Gardner who had a great deal of experience working with Christian occult groups and Freemasons in the 1930s and 40s. This included groups linked to the Rosicrucians and to the Co-masons, a form of masonry which allowed women to join.

Gardner was given the position of 'resident witch' of Williamson's Witchcraft Museum and as a result came into contact with a large number of people who were interested in witchcraft. Gradually the form of practice that was developed by Gerald Gardner spread and became a significant force in the Witchcraft community, ultimately becoming known as Gardnerianism which led to the development of a number of other forms of practice.

Whilst these developments were taking place other witches, who derived their practice directly from traditional witchcraft, appeared. Ultimately these witches have, to a significant extent, gathered under the banner of the foremost practitioner of this tradition in the 20th Century, Robert Cochrane. Cochrane was a draughtsman from Slough to the west of London and unlike Gardener who was from the elite he was a member of a working class family. He was, however, extremely intelligent and thoroughly researched witchcraft in the early 60s.

Cochrane created a structure that has proved enduring, particularly due to the members of the coven that he recruited. Foremost amongst these was Ron White who went on to found the Regency, a group which created structures that resolve many of the issues that Witchcraft groups face. Robert Cochrane's coven had also promoted the Wiccan Rede in 1964. The Rede became the primary philosophy of the spiritual practice of Wicca which developed after Gardner's death, and living according to The Wiccan Rede is an aspiration of many modern witches.

When we look at the practice of a coven we need to determine which type of coven we are dealing with. Is it one in the Cochranian style or is it in the Gardenerian form. Of course there are many covens that are only loosely associated with one or other of these forms, however in almost all cases covens either follow the ceremonial magic of the Gardnerian tradition or derive their practice from traditional witchcraft directly often through the Cochrane tradition.

The primary difference between the two practices is that Gardnerianism is a highly ceremonial form of practice that involves skyclad working, where the practitioners are initiated without clothing. The Cochranian tradition is strongly based on the use of robes, often identical, to create a feeling of equality. This contrasts strongly with the Gardnerian Tradition which is hierarchical and where in the novice can only be inducted into the tradition by those with the relevant higher level initiation themselves. This contrasts with Cochranianism where there is only one level of initiation.

When forming a coven it is of course necessary to determine which type of practice is going to take place. Cochranian covens are typically more accessible and have a richer network of covens on the ground. Gardnerian networks can be fragmentary and hard to access, however they can be found. As a result it is more straightforward to consider the forming of a coven in the Cochranian style.

2. What does a coven do ?

At the heart of coven practice is a monthly gathering at the full moon which is termed a sabbat. At this gathering the members of the coven stand in a circle and call the four elements of earth, air, fire and water. They then perform magic and share the sacrament of cakes and ale or bread and wine

There are many other practices that take place inside the magic circle when it is formed on a monthly basis. These include readings, scrying, knot work and a range of other activities which may be arranged by the Maiden or Magister running the rite.

Before the rite takes place there is often a chance for coven members to chat and catch up on activities over the last month. They also typically share information about the wider Wiccan and pagan community. After the rite takes place there is typically an opportunity for members of the coven to eat together. Sometimes this takes the form of a sit-down meal and on other occasions it could be a more informal arrangement when members bring food and share it with others from the coven. So there is far more to a sabat than simply the casting of a ritual circle and the other aspects of coven activity are extremely important.

A further highly important element of a Wiccan coven is training. Although there are covens that do not train their members it is extremely difficult in practice to grow a coven without a strong training program. This training typically leads the individual to an initiation into the practice. Some of the training takes place before the initiation but additional training typically also takes place after it.

The structure of this training is very dependent on the Maiden or Magister running the coven. Within the Gardnerian tradition it is common for the student to be given tasks to perform and then close to the initiation to write up their Book of Shadows, or grimoire, which includes copying the Gardnerian rites

The Cochranian based traditions are different and typically have highly structured and long courses, often running over three years. These courses involve the study of a wide range of practices. These include different forms of magic including crystal magic, the study of trees, the study of the history of their own tradition and a wide range of other aspects of Witchcraft practice. This is not always the case, however. Some covens offer very little training which may be produced on a more ad-hoc basis by Maiden or Magister of the coven.

There are many different ways that covens run. Some only meet on the full moon. Others meet on the sabbats of the solar cycle, which include the solstices and equinoxes and four other festivals called the cross quarters, which include Halloween and Lammas.

Although covens are focused on full moon rituals many will meet in between the full moon gatherings. Some will meet for a new Moon right however it is far more common for the coven to meet informally for coffee or drinks or to chat over ideas for the next sabbat and this may not include all of the members of the coven. This will depend on their availability and the distance they need to travel to get the coven meetings. These meetings will typically take place in a coffee shop, pub or even in the house of a member.

Many covens also have WhatsApp groups in which coven members will share what they are doing and when they produce material or come up with ideas related to their practice it will often be shared with members of the group. Many Wiccans also trade with each other and help each other in their businesses. The coven also acts as a support structure for those who are interested in ritual practice.

In addition to the regular cycle, built around the full moon sabbats, covens also often visit other areas for example on day trips or even for a more extended holiday. Typical destinations for the longest trips include Glastonbury and Dartmoor, which is a particularly beautiful spot for ritual practice. Covens will often simply come up with ideas of places to go together. When there they may visit other covens from the local area that are connected with their tradition.

An example of this was a trip organised by a London based covering to visit the Stiperstones in Shropshire, which is an important site in the Cochrane tradition. It was the working site of Ron White, the lead of the Regency after he left London in the mid 1970s to live in Church Stretton in Shropshire. The London coven had close connections with a coven in Birmingham and arranged to meet them at the site for a ritual and also for a drink. The Coven also visited Salisbury and ate together by the river.

This type of practice is extremely enjoyable and goes some way to explain the durability of covens. Certainly anyone forming a coven will benefit from socialising with their coven and sharing time with them. Trips to Dartmoor also provide a great opportunity for the sharing of memorable experiences and beautiful ritual practice with other Wiccans.

3. Why form a coven

The primary reason for forming a coven is to perform magic in a group. The reason to perform this magic is to achieve the thing that a Wiccan wants to achieve. At a deeper level to be able to achieve the things that we want to achieve, to fulfil our true will, is to connect oneself with our ingenious spirit, our true will. If we are unable to achieve the things we wish to achieve we will generally end up being controlled by others.

Covens offer an advantage over working solitary in this regard. The first advantage is that they offer a chance to avoid working magic in an echo chamber where no reliable criticism is possible. Other coven members will help with the working of the spell to achieve a member's true will. The second advantage is that they can offer divination, including tarot readings, to deal with the psychological aspects of the individual's wish.

In the public sphere tarot readings of any quality are expensive. In covens they will often be free, and may be more relevant. Additionally a pair of coven members can read for each other. This 'pair reading' option does not easily exist outside a coven environment. So ultimately covens offer freedom by achieving your will.

There are many aspects to working magic. One of the key issues is that in order for magic to be effective a magical environment is helpful. Covens work together to create a magical feeling when they gather for their full moon rituals. Coven training should also provide some background in how religious groups operate. This can act to control or free the members. Many religious groups control their members and are expensive to be part of. Although they offer support to their members this may be at the expense of personal freedom. Wiccan groups provide a community but are less prone to controlling the freedom of their members.

It is important to remember that Wicca is not for everybody. Some people do not seek freedom or to follow their own individual desire. Some prefer working in large groups which provide them with instruction on how to live their life. Some people simply don't have a clear idea of what they want to do and are happy to be led by others. But for those who have a strong idea of their own will and what they are looking to achieve, for them being a member of a Wiccan coven can be very beneficial.

Although the social aspects are important they are not the driving force behind a coven. The main driver is to be able to engage in a spiritual practice of magic with other people. For those looking to set up covens it is important that there is a strong focus at the centre on ritual, magic working, divination through tarot or other means and the study of the traditions which facilitate this.

In practice this means offering training. This training will cover the background to Wicca but also show the working of magic, the performance of ritual and using tarot and other means for divination. This provides the key focus for any coven that is formed

4. Connecting yourself to the community

An individual looking to form a coven will first typically connect themselves to the local Wiccan and pagan community. This is because it is necessary to recruit members for the coven and these are likely to be found in part in these types of groups. Some covens form very quickly from groups of friends, however an individual looking to form a coven will not necessarily find it easy at first to find the people who will form the membership of the coven. But those who wish to join covens do exist and with effort they can be found. Nonetheless the coven may soon flounder if structured training is not available for the members as they join.

It is helpful for an individual to keep their eyes open for a shortcut to form in a coven where a group of practitioners assemble spontaneously. It is also important, however, that if this does not happen a Wiccan looking to put together a coven for ritual practice should prepare themselves prior to actively seeking membership of the coven itself.

This preparation consists of main elements. Firstly the Wiccan needs to connect with the local community. Secondly they need to develop a full set of training material so that they are able to offer those joining the coven or way to learn the tradition. Thirdly they need to establish their practice very firmly so that when they bring people into that covering they are clear about what they are doing in terms of ritual practice.

The most important aspect of a Wiccan group is therefore ritual practice and it is vital that the Maiden or Magister leading the rite has a strong capability in the performance of Wiccan rites. This is strongly aided by a clear understanding on behalf of the Wiccan looking to leave a coven about the type of practice they want to follow.

Specifically the need to determine whether they want to create a coven which is based on the ideas of traditional witchcraft or whether they want to follow the ceremonial magic and highly tiered structure of Gardnerianism and the Golden Dawn. Once an individual has a good set of connections in the local pagan community they will need to create a training course to offer a good understanding of the ritual practice they want to perform they will be ready to form a coven.

5. Finding a lineage

When forming a coven a group identity is very important. In order to survive the coven needs to have a reason for its existence. There are two main approaches that people take when forming a Wiccan or Witchcraft Coven. These can be termed eclectic or tradition based. If the coven is planning to take its inspiration from a wide range of sources it would be termed eclectic. If, on the other hand, it draws its inspiration from a particular type of practice it will follow one of the pre-existing traditions. There are many of these including Corellian, Gardnerian, Alexandrian, Cochranian and Dianic. These traditions all have their particular emphasis or way of working.

Covens that are eclectic and draw together a wide range of traditions are generally led by individuals with a very clear personal idea of their practice. One trend that is seen is the mixing of Buddhist ideas within Wicca. Those seeking to mix native British traditions with ideas from Buddhism are likely to have a very clear understanding of both British Witchcraft and Buddhist traditions. For them the merging of these two traditions is a natural way to harness the power of both. It is worth recognising however that for many who look to practice traditional witchcraft the incorporation of Buddhist elements will not be attractive and therefore it may be best not to incorporate this approach in the early stages of coven practice.

If the founder is keen to mix traditions and build a practice that incorporates chakra work, reincarnation, Nordic practice, yoga or huna then it is likely that they will form an eclectic group. If they do this the pathway is simple. They can simply plan to form your coven and are likely to find your place in the wider Wiccan community.

There will be some who will not acknowledge this practice as 'true Wicca'. This will often be because the coven is not a member of their tradition and they feel that theirs is the 'true' one. This problem is not unique to Wicca. Christian also sometimes don't share communion with other Christian groups, and may even not view them as true believers. Eclectic Wiccans should not be concerned by the judgement of others and should press ahead with the formation of the coven in the style that the wish to follow

In general Wiccans following this approach typically find this criticism a minor issue. Additionally any Wiccan may face the same issue and not be accepted by other groups. Gardnerians may find their practice criticised as a recent innovation and Cochranians may not be accepted by Gardnerians. Trying to resolve these types of criticism is unhelpful and the individual leading the coven should press ahead with creating the type of practice that is right for them.

Is worth being aware, however, of the fact that many covens have been set up on an eclectic basis but have folded after a few meetings because there isn't enough depth within the practice for the tradition to endure. In order for this approach to be effective the founder of the coven will need to have a clear idea of their own practice and it may be worthwhile to document this in a training course to establish a strong group identity. If this doesn't happen it is likely that the coven will not succeed without a very strong figurehead, and even that may not be enough.

In some cases the establishment of an eclectic coven has been seen as a shortcut or a quick way to establish a ritual group. In practice this is not the case and although eclectic ovens can work very well they need, to an even greater extent than those based on Traditional Witchcraft or Gardnerianism, to have strong training courses and to be very clear the practice that they seek to follow.

The second approach is to connect with one of the existing lineages or or trends within the broader witchcraft movement. Many of the lineages exist to carry on the ideas of their founder, however some are also part of broader social movements which can give them additional strength. The reason why lineages are often based on the ideas of a founder who leaves written texts is because the initiates of these traditions value the opinions of those who have developed the practice.

This is not however the only driver which keeps covens together for long periods. Some covens seek to maintain the worship of the divine feminine. Others bind together those of particular sexual orientations. Without something to bind the group it is hard for it to survive. In the case of the Old Horse Wiccans the coven exists to maintain a lineaged connection to the original Witchcraft, to the Old Faith. To those within the tradition this is of great importance, because to imagine that there is no genuine connection to the Old Faith appears to their initiates to be a great loss. For others this simply isn't important. For them to worship in a feminist enpowered setting, revering to a divine mother is of great importance. Neither of these are right or wrong but they are both of great importance to the durability of these traditions.

When a coven is established this central theme is required. Around this needs to be built a culture in which all of the actions, rituals and tools are congruent with this basic belief. This connection with a thread of Witchcraft needs therefore to be the starting point.

When a coven is breaking away from another tradition much of this work has been done. If, for example, a coven is breaking away within the Gardnerian tradition they will base much of their practice on the work of Gerald Gardner. If, on the other hand, the breakaway is from a Dianic Wiccan coven the practice will be based on Dianic traditions.

For those who are seeking to start a coven from scratch it is vital that this mythos, this link to the past, is understood if the coven is to have the maximum chance of survival in the long run and there are many options. Those who are interested in the green movement are often drawn to Wicca. There has been an emerging trend for Green Wicca to emerge out of this, however there is little in the way of formal practice. This tradition appears to be partly rooted in the old ideas of herbal magic and the wise woman. One of the most prominent Wiccans, Scott Cunningham, had a great knowledge of herbal lore and published an important encyclopaedia on this topic. It would certainly be possible to build a tradition out of his ideas and those related to it. In this case however it would be beneficial to seek out an individual who has a personal connection with these traditions rather than simply using texts.

Others have focused on the Cunning Man tradition. In this case there are also people with links to these practices. From these it is possible that traditions can be built which acquire over time acquire great skill in these practices. This is an approach which is more likely to lead to a strong long-term coven than simply acquiring a mix of eclectic traditions. Of course it is still possible to build a a practice in an eclectic form however it would be likely to require a very able and charismatic individual to sustain a group on this basis.

Where a coven seeks to connect with an existing tradition but does not have a lineage from it there are options. Many of the major traditions have published material which has been specifically created to help those looking to practice the tradition outside the lineaged pathways.

In the case of those interested in the Cochranian tradition there is an important book 'Witchcraft a tradition Renewed' by Evan John Jones and Doreen Valiente. This book provides a good basis of rites and practices that are linked to Modern Traditional Witchcraft. This book is specifically designed to help those establishing current practice in a Cochranian format.

For those interested in the Alexandrian tradition there is another text, 'The Witches' Bible', which contains many of the rights required to run a coven. These provide a way for individuals to set up a Wiccan tradition that, although not directly lineaged to one of these traditions, can operate as a stream of it. It is worth bearing in mind that Alex Sanders himself was a first degree initiate of Gardnerianism and although he claimed some family practice this is not universally accepted. Despite this he established a very strong line of practice and there is no reason why a new coven could not establish its practice based on this book. Additionally once established a coven using the Alexandrian format may come into contact with an initiated Alexandrian who will provide them with the lineage if they feel this is necessary. The key is to have a strong and meaningful spiritual practice and a dedicated commitment to the path. This will be sufficient to maintain a coven whereas a lineaged group without dedication and commitment to the path will generally fail to endure.

The most likely reason for someone to set up a new tradition that is a stream of an older one is that they are in an area where there simply are no covens. In the case of any tradition once a group is established it may be that someone will appear who has a direct link to that tradition and they may help establish a formal connection with it. If that opportunity does not arise it is likely to be an indication that the tradition is very much closed to new members and as a result the newly established stream of that practice is likely to draw in those who cannot access it due to location or for other reasons. Either way it is better to get started then wait for the approval of someone else which may not arrive.

In order to select a tradition on which to base a coven it is important to be aware of the main existing traditions. There are advantages and disadvantages to each of them.

It is also helpful to understand the main themes within witchcraft from which covens are likely to be drawn.

Wiccan Traditions

The following are a list of traditions that may provide inspiration for those looking to establish their own coven. This is not a full list, however it covers the main types of Wicca. Other Wiccan traditions are likely to be derived from, or closely related to, one of these traditions.

Alexandrian Wicca

Alexandrian Wicca is a tradition that was founded by Alex Sanders in the 1960a. The word Alexandrian is said to refer to the city of Alexandria rather than to Alex Sanders himself and to reflect a practice of using a wide range of traditions from various sources based on whether they are effective or not.

Alexandrian practices are closely aligned to those of Gerald Gardner. This is understood to be because the rituals themselves are taken from a copy of Gardener's Book of Shadows. Since Alex Sanders was a first-degree initiate it is logical that this is the case.

Those looking to practise Alexandrian Wicca would often see Gardnerian Wicca as an alternative. One of the problems with Gardnerian practice however is that Gerald Gardner made a number of comments that are unacceptable in the modern era and as a result Alexandrian practice may be a better alternative for those who otherwise would practise Gardnarianism. It is a way of practising in a Gardnerian style without taking on board all of the ideas of Gardener and it allows for a more independent way of thinking about a tradition that is otherwise appealing but has issues with the views of its founder.

Alexandrian Wicca uses skyclad initiations and can incorporate scourging and binding of the initiate. Although these practices may be off putting to some for others they are a vital active ingredient of Wiccan practice. As a result Alexandrianism provides an alternative for those who wish to practise in this style but not associated with some of the ideas of Gerald Gardner.

Chaos Magic

Chaos magic originates in Britain and has as an important text, Liber Null, by Peter Caroll. The tradition uses a range of techniques that many have found to be effective. There is no Wiccan tradition evident currently that uses Chaos Magic however there is some crossover in ideas between Chaos Magic and the way that Wicca is practised in some traditions.

Cochranian Wicca

Cochranian Wicca is a Wiccan tradition that is inspired by the ideas of Robert Cochrane. It claims a stream of the Cochranian tradition through and informed by Ron White and George Stannard's ritual practice as The Regency. It uses the Regency sites in London and elsewhere as its main ritual centres. Some Cochranian Wiccans also claim a lineaged connection to the Old Faith which is rare amongst Wiccan groups.

The practice of Cochranianism itself is very broad and incorporates a large number of traditions. It has also been influential in many related traditions. One of the key points about the Cochranian tradition is that in the immediate aftermath of the death of Cochrane Ron White, the leader of the Regency, determined that in order to form a coven in the Cochranian tradition it was necessary to follow a series of steps that show the dedication of the individual and and that the individual should be connected to other practitioners.

One of the main differences between Cochranian practice and other forms of Wicca is that Cochranianism is very much a group based practice. In the case of Gardnarianism the lineage has, on occasions, been passed from one person to another outside of a coven practice, and Gardner himself was known to perform this. This approach is, however, not common in Cochranian practice.

The writings of many of the individuals who followed from Robert Cochrane state that a coven should be formed in order to practise. This is clear in the writings of Evan John Jones and Ron White. The emphasis is on the dedication of the individual and the performance of particular tasks including writing and performing rituals and creating a group. This is not to say that initiations are not very important within Cochranian practice, but these initiations take place within newly formed covens and bind together those individuals in them and those who join them. Ron White specifically excluded the possibility of lineaged initiation through The Regency. It is understood that this was to encourage the formation of new covens and this has certainly been the effect of his approach.

As a result Cochranians value their personal connections with other other Cochranians who have themselves personal links that go back to Robert Cochranee. Cochranian practice, however, generally requires a coven and simply having a close link to another Cochranian initiate is not generally, on its own, relevant for those practising Cochranian Wicca.

For those looking to practise Cochranian Wicca, therefore, the key elements are to be a Cochranian, meaning to accept the the ideas of Cochrane as the basis for coven practice, and to be a Wiccan i.e. to follow the Wiccan Rede. Also the formation of a coven is generally central and practised. The commonly used elements include the use of stang within the practice, the creation of the magic circle as a castle, the use of black robes and a reverence for the ideas of British Traditional Witchcraft. There are many texts including the letters of Robert Cochrane that are used in this practice.

These are the key elements rather than requiring a lineage from another Cochranian Wiccan group. Nonetheless having a stream or lineage to other Cochranian Wiccan covens is desirable to many. It is not, however, essential as long as a coven with three members is formed that is true to the practice. Solitary initiation does not, however, form part of Cochranian Wiccan practice as envisaged by Ron White or Evan John Jones, the two main streams of practice that emerged from the Thames Valley Coven after Cochrane's death.

There are lines of solitary practice that have emerged that have links to Cochranian practice but they do not generally describe themselves as Wiccan. As a result Cochranian Wicca is a good option for those who are looking to establish a coven that is tied to the ideas of Traditional Witchcraft rather than ceremonial magic and do not wish to practise on a solitary basis.

Correllian Wicca

Correllian Wicca is a Wiccan tradition that is based in North America and contains within it elements of Native American practice. The Correllians provide training and are known for being an accessible tradition for those wishing to practise.

The links of Correllian practice to nativist traditions will be appealing to some, particularly those in North America. Corellian practice is also very structured and this allows an individual to use this material to train themselves and others. Given the importance of training in the establishment of Wiccan covens this may be helpful.

In the case of Correllian Wicca it may also be possible to find people online to train in the practice. The online training of Correllian Wicca legitimises it for those who feel that this is necessary. So Correllianism is a good option for those who want a direct connection with a practice and may want to start practising on a solitary basis before establishing a coven practice.

Cunning Man Traditions

The Cunning Man tradition is a practice which has a long history. Cunning men were workers of magic. Within the practice there is a long tradition of solitary practice however is involved in the tradition may switch between solitary and coven practice. As a result this tradition is useful for someone in a remote area who may find it difficult to establish a coven but over a long period of time will find local practitioners that they can work with.

Dianic Wicca

Dianic Wicca is one of the major traditions of Wiccan practice. The Dianics are understood to be the first to have used Wicca to describe their tradition. Dianic Wicca is a tradition that emphasises the Divine feminine and may incorporate a monotheistic approach. They may also only accept women into the practice. The tradition is closely associated with the broader feminist movement.

There are traditions that are linked to the Dianics that accept men into practice however many who would seek to establish Dianic covens would not accept men into the practice. This is restrictive in a situation where a coven is looking to commence Wiccan practice and some of those interested may be men.

Those who are drawn to Dianic Wicca are generally very clear about the type of practice they are looking for and are unlikely to compromise in the type of practice that they're looking to set up. For those interested in setting up a coven in this style the works of Zsuzsanna Budapest are the best starting point.

Faery Wicca

Faery Wicca is a Wiccan tradition that emphasises the importance of fairies. It is a good option for those who are drawn to fairy practice or experience fairies within their life. Generally these types of covens are smaller and form on a more ad hoc basis than other traditions.

Gardnerian Wicca

Gardnerian Wicca is one of the most prominent of the Wiccan traditions. Gardnerianism was established in the 1950s and is a practice that is based on ceremonial magic. Large elements of Gardnerian practice are understood to derive from the Golden Dawn, Aleister Crowley and Rosicrucianism.

Gardnerian Wicca is a good option for those who are looking to be involved in a practice that sees itself as the standard form of Wicca. It has many of the elements associated with Wiccan practice including skyclad working, scourging and binding of the initiates.

There are a number of problems in practice with establishing a Gardnerian coven. The main one is that if a coven is being established from scratch, incorporating new members, then skyclad practice complicates the process greatly and may delay or even prevent a coven from forming.

Gardnerians can be inflexible in in what they accept as legitimate coven and as a result failure to initiate on a skyclad basis may cause dissent from other groups, however many Gardnerian covens have practised in this way and if a Gardnerian coven is being formed it may be more practical in the first case to initiate coven members incorporating tokenistic elements of the skyclad practice rather than full ritual nudity.

A further issue is that Gardnerians typically have a requirement for a lineaged initiation meaning that is necessary to initiate into a Gardnerian coven. This is not always the case and there have been examples of Gardnerian groups establishing without a lineage but this may cause conflict with other Gardnerians. Alexandrianism is arguably a case of a Gardnerian derived tradition although to many outsiders it is indistinguishable from Gradnerianism and the term Al/Gard may be used to define these.

One of the reasons why some wish to initiate into Gardnerianism is that some Gardnerians deny that other forms of Wicca are legitimate, even Alexandrianism and they may seek to avoid this criticism. This has, however, been less common in recent years. One of the key reasons for this is the release of research backed up by Google Ngrams that show that the Wiccan Rede, the central philosophy of Wicca, originates in Cochranianism. This understanding is backed up by knowledge of the events of the mid 1960s held within Cochranian networks. Nonetheless some seek Gardnerianism as a mainstream Wiccan practice.

A final issue to be considered is that Gerald Gardener is known to have made comments which were homophobic. Few seeking to establish a Gardnerian coven would wish to be associated with the views and this can potentially lead to criticism. Others are unhappy about the ardanes or old laws of Gardnerianism which prefer younger women over older women as High Priestesses. As a result it is likely that Gardnerian covens will be required to reject these ideas and as a result pure Gardnerianism is uncommon. Nonetheless Gardnerianism remains a major force within Wicca and is likely to be considered as a form of Wicca by those looking to establish a coven.

Green Wicca

Green Wicca is the name given to traditions of Wicca that emphasise the green movement. Green Wicca is a relatively recent phenomenon, although many Wiccans have been attracted to the green movement. Green Wiccans tend to place very little emphasis on lineage and far more on a style of practice and this can also incorporate solitary working. As a result Green Wicca is potentially a good approach for someone looking to build a coven from scratch without any connections to other Wiccans.

Golden Dawn Traditions

The Golden Dawn was a network of magicians that existed in the early part of the 20th century. This tradition left a vast amount of material which can be used to create ritual practice. Many Wiccan traditions draw some of their practice from the Golden Dawn.

The Golden Dawn does have ritual groups however is not seen as a form of Wicca, rather as a pool of information from which a Wiccan practice can be created. As a result building a coven based on Golden Dawn material is likely to be a good option for someone looking to create a practice from scratch rather than working with an existing form of Wicca.

Old Horse Traditions

The Old Horse traditions are a range of shamanistic practices that is seen around the UK. These practices are seen to be the remnant of the true spiritual practice of the past and integrally connected with witchcraft. There are many records of the Old Horse traditions being banned by the church. The traditions will typically appeal to those who seek a direct connection with Witchcraft within their practice.

The Old Horse tradition is connected to Cochranianism since Robert Cochrane defined the stang as 'the horse'. This is because the fork of the stang can be used to carry the skull of a horse or deer. It emphasises a lineaged connection to the Old Faith and the importance of the horse pole. There are a network of Old Horse Covens in the South of England

Streams and Lineages

Where a Wiccan is drawn to practice in alignment with one of the existing traditions there are a number of significant issues. As a result the individuals forming the coven will need to understand the way that the Wiccan community works with regards to its existing traditions.

Within Wicca there are two forms of connection with previous traditions. The first of these is termed a lineage. This is where an individual has an lineaged, or direct, connection to the prior tradition. The second is a stream. A stream has knowledge of a lineaged tradition but isn't directly lineaged to it, it is inspired by a tradition.

Generally the membership of a lineage is initiatory. If an individual Wiccan hasn't been initiated into that tradition then they will generally not be accepted as Wiccans of that lineage. In this case, if an individual is unable to find a coven which is connected to the tradition to which you wish to connect, or if there are no spaces you will need to take a different approach. Generally an individual will wish to connect with a tradition for a particular reason. A common case is women wishing to be a Dianic Wiccan and practice with other women.

The key issue is that different traditions place a different emphasis on lineages. In the case of Cochranianism the creation of a coven is the most important aspect and covens in the Cochranian tradition will typically accept the legitimacy of other Cochranian covens even if they are not connected to their lineage directly. There are exceptions to this, the primary one being where the Cochranian group is run by a Gardnerian initiate, but problems with recognition of a coven's legitimacy are unlikely in the case of the non Gardnerian initiates connected within Cochranianism. This approach is largely a result of the teachings of Ron White and the recognition of the fact that the Wiccan Rede, which is aligned to this approach, originates in Cochranianism.

In the case of Gardnerianism forming a coven in a Gardnerian format without an initiatory link to the practice is likely to cause conflict with other groups. It is unlikely that this will prevent the coven from running however if the coven grows to a reasonable size it may cause difficulties and this needs to be considered when forming a coven. The same problem may occur when forming an Alexandrian Coven. The problem may be less severe in this case however the difficulties that this may cause for a new coven should be considered.

It is possible to create a new coven with no direct or indirect links to any other tradition. In this way a new Wiccan tradition is formed. All of the major traditions have to some extent been created in this way and the emergence of Green Wicca is an indication that this process may continue.

A new tradition may be inspired by another tradition but will be a tradition in its own right. There have been many examples of people doing this in the past as nobody owns the word Wicca. If your coven is effective this is likely to draw the attention of members of other traditions. You may be offered an initiation into a longer established tradition. If the coven wishes it can then merge its tradition into another lineage and gain an initiation into the tradition that was hard to access. But more likely a new but established form of Wicca will find its place in the wider Wiccan community and new forms of Wicca seem certain to appear in the future.

6. Creating a grimoire and assembling tools

In order to establish a coven it is necessary to have a Grimoire with the rituals within it and also a series of tools used to perform the rituals of Witchcraft. Many Witchcraft lineages have their own rites which are used by practitioners, however these are typically insufficient for full practice and it is therefore necessary for those running covens to have their own material.

Writing a grimoire is complex and time consuming if it is to be meaningful and to create beautiful rites. It is best therefore to work on this material prior to forming the ritual group which will be the precursor to the coven. Once the formation of a ritual group has been announced this will set in process a series of events which will constrain the ability of the Maiden, Magister or HP/HPs leading the coven to delay. As a result it is important to deal with as many of the typical aspects of ritual practice as possible prior to announcing the formation of the coven. it is therefore necessary to consider the key aspects of practice to be used prior to advertising for members.

Robes

Robes are a very important aspect of coven practice. Even those covens that are predominantly skyclad will sometimes use robes. There are three main approaches to the use of robes. The first approach is that everybody purchases their own robes. If this happens there may be many different robes in use and typically the leader of the coven may have a better robe than the other members. Some members may want to use robes that are not designed for use in covens, for example those for martial arts groups or those for general use. The second approach is to not use robes. The final approach is to have a set of matching robes for the whole coven.

Although it is expensive to purchase a full set of robes it is one of the most important investments that someone running a coven can make. Without a full set of robes Wiccan practice loses a key aspect. It is possible to practise with a variety of different robes and some covens can sustain their practice on that basis, however the impression given is not as strong as as with matching set

Covens that have no robes at all rarely survive. This is because it is an indication that the participants are not serious and also because robes create a magical atmosphere which is appealing and which encourages new members to practise on a regular basis.

Getting hold of a set of robes can be difficult. It is possible to make your own robes. Some covens have a practice of forcing trainees, as part of their training, to make a robe, however this rarely leads to an attractive robe being produced. It is possible to make a simple poncho however this doesn't give the impression associated with Witchcraft.

Where covens are fortunate enough to have a member who is a skilled seamstress or tailor it is possible for them to make their own robes from scratch. To do this the purchase of a pattern will be required. There are some significant benefits in a coven making its own robes. The first of these is that it is easier to replace a robe that is damaged or lost with one that is identical. Secondly it is possible to create a unique robe from a pattern that ensures that the robes of the coven will not be seen elsewhere. The problem is is that the coven may be dependent on on the the person making the robes and if they are not reliable, or leave the coven, then it will be almost impossible to get matching robes

The next option is to purchase a set of robes. These can be purchased from eBay or Amazon. There are a wide selection of styles and colours available and the purchase of a set is straightforward. The main problem that is faced is that over time suppliers change and it may not be possible to replace missing robes and ultimately an entirely new set may need to be purchased at a cost of several hundred pounds. Additionally other Wiccans may have the same robe so it will not be unique however this can be solved by the use of cords, patches or other methods. Despite the drawbacks this is the simplest and most practical approach for coven and as a bare minimum four matching robes should be purchased or made.

Writing a grimoire

The second aspect of practice that should be considered in detail prior to the announcement of the initial ritual group is the creation of grimoire. This itself is a long and difficult process, which will only be completed after the coven is up in running.

It is important to have a grimoire cover that has pages that can be removed since there will be a requirement to add and modify it on a regular basis. One of the best options is to use a wood covered book with removable pins that allows for the addition and removal of material. These books have a beautiful feel to them and in addition to being extremely functional are used by a number of Wiccan and Witchcraft groups.

The basic form of rite for the stream or lineage which is used to create the coven should be assembled in this and the key problems of initiating the coven in the and the first members should be dealt with. The different levels of initiation and dedication and the closing of the initiatory cycle all need to be dealt with. This should be done as early as possible so that before the first meeting takes place the Magister, Maiden or HP/HPs leading the coven has a clear idea what they're trying to achieve.

Once the process of forming that coven has been started decisions will be made that may be difficult to change later. As a result it is very important to have a clear vision about the final form of the coven in terms of its practice and to work from the beginning towards that. Without having a complete grimoire it is difficult to do this.

7. Creating a training course

The development of a training course is one of the key aspects that will determine the success or failure of a coven. It is extremely difficult to produce strong training material. Typically a good deal of study and organisation by the person running the coven will be required.

It is possible to use a Gardnerian style approach where tasks are simply given to the novice, however in the Cochranian tradition or Traditional Witchcraft this does not reflect the norms of the practice. This is because knowledge is at the heart of the quest of many who evolved in these practices and as a result a course where they are forced to do their own study on a self study basis is unlikely to hold the members in the training cause and will weaken the coven in the long run.

The importance of training for a functioning Wiccan coven cannot be overstated. Many people try to start covens and find later that the production and running of training is onerous and difficult and as a result the training ends and the coven soon breaks up. It has been repeatedly seen that many of the leaders of successful covens often have a background in teaching and have university based teacher training. This provides a great deal of experience in producing lessons under pressure and a short notice and as a result those with this knowledge are able to deal with the requirement for a structured training course which is typically the single most important element when forming a strong ritual practice.

Designing a course

The first stage of creating the course is to design the format which it is going to be used. Typically within Cochranian covens the training is broken down into blocks of thirteen lessons. These lessons take many forms. They may be a series of lectures which are given by the Magister of the Coven to the novices. Alternatively they may be written and then printed off and given to the students to complete. Where the second option takes place however the tasks that are given are typically supported by a large amount of written information. It is not effective to simply provide references to read particular books or to leave the student to complete the work on their own.

The most powerful types of courses are those that have been written in advance by the Maiden or Magister of the coven and then delivered in person to the novices. This training may take the form of trips to particular sites that are important to Wiccans or which illustrate aspects of Wiccan practice. Alternatively they may take the form of study in the front room of the Maiden, Magister or HP/HPs where they are taught the fundamentals of Wiccan theory and practice

Homework

One of the key elements of many Wiccan courses is the homework that takes place. Typically the novice will be given work to complete and sometimes this may be tested in the lesson itself. Alternatively the work may be required to be written by the initiate to be marked by the Maiden, Magister or HP/HPs.

When building a good course it is vital to consider all aspects, for example to ensure that homework is available for every lesson. The written material which is going to be used within the practice needs to be of a high standard. It is also important to decide how the material that has been studied will be tested to ensure that the students have understood what they have been taught. So there are a wide range of considerations for someone putting together a course. Once the novices have started on the course the person training them will be very busy and will struggle to find time to develop more aspects of the course.

Experience is also shown that if the person producing the course is not a trained teacher it can be very difficult for them to put together a course and even when they do it is not pleasant for them to do so because they are dealing with something that is very unfamiliar. For this reason it is doubly important for those without a background in teaching to complete the course before the start to recruit members. This may not be the preferred option since it is a challenging task, however failure to do so may lead to the later collapse of the coven so it is of great importance to address this issue.

Pre and post initiation

One aspect which is worth considering is the fact that there is different training before and after initiation. The pre-initiation training typically involves learning the fundamentals and only exposes the novice to the specific traditions of the coven to a limited extent. After the initiation has taken place the student is a full member of the coven and more detailed knowledge and information will be revealed to them.

It is very important to have the pre-initiation training fully completed prior to the establishment of the coven. It is also important to not ignore the requirement for the training of the coven members post initiation, and significant thought must be given from the very start about the overall structure of the entire course.

8. Committing to starting a coven

Initially the formation of the coven can be put off however ultimately the time will come when the decision to create the coven is made. This commitment will lead to a shift in the way that the Maiden, Magister or HP/HPs who will form the coven works with the outside world and the extent to which their ideas and the information about the proposed coven formation are presented to those who may potentially join.

In the early stages of coven formation it is not helpful to announce the plan to form a coven. The reason for this is that within any Wiccan community there will be existing ritual groups and these will typically not recognise other groups and may seek to hinder their development. This may cause conflict and as a result is it best to to leave the announcing of a coven until the time when it is necessary to do so.

Engaging with the issue of announcing the formation of a ritual group is something that should be left as long as possible. The point when it is necessary is when the individual forming the coven needs to form groups which have structures which can lead people into coven practice. At this point an individual taking this action may find themselves in conflict with others in their own community. This can lead, for example, to them being unwelcome at some public events. As a result this is an important step away from theoretical planning to actual practice which can make a difference to the spiritual path of the individual. There is, however, no alternative and at some point this step will be required to be taken.

The first step will typically be the formation of a public presence through groups like Facebook, Instagram, Meetup or simply a webpage which announces the formation of a group which will engage in ritual practice. Once this group or social network is connected with recruitment then, if this is successful, the possibility of a coven being formed becomes much closer to a reality. This means that the individual forming the coven should be well organised prior to them taking the step.

The biggest issue in the early stages of coven formation is the recruitment of members. On the other hand those who have sought to join Wiccan covens frequently report that it is extremely difficult to access a good Wiccan coven. This is because the Wiccan groups are voluntary organisations and often are disorganised. For this reason it is important from the beginning to have structures which are well organised especially in regards to bringing in new members.

One of the key aspects of this is that when a person contacts the network the person leading the group must respond to them and make it easy for them to communicate with the network promptly and without any undue inconvenience in the process. This means, for example, that a person who seeks to join a coven's digital groups should be connected as quickly as possible and be made to feel welcome.

If they seek to join a physical group meeting in public it should be made clear where the meeting is and how to contact the organiser when the new member arrives. People joining Wiccan networks often feel that they may not be welcome and as a result are sensitive to a failure to connect quickly, which they may view as a sign that they are not welcome. For this reason it is important to be very careful how new contacts are dealt with and how meetings are set up.

It might be felt that checking all of the contact points weekly would be sufficient, however progress will be greatly sped up if this is done daily until the point at which the task of monitoring the new members can be handed over to a third party. The fact that this is important is one of the reasons why it is so difficult for coven organisers to sustain the effort required to recruit members to a coven. It does, however, mean that if an individual continues to make a sustained effort over a long period they are likely to be successful.

The main issues to watch out for are firstly offering access to a digital network but failing to respond in a timely way to people who enquire about joining it. If an enquiry is made and a month later a response given the member may have found another group or lost interest. The second problem is arranging face-to-face meetings and then not making it possible for attendees to find the organiser. One coven, which had many new members applying to it, met monthly in Wetherspoons.The problem was that they didn't issue a phone number and new members were forced to ask around tables in a large pub to find the coven. Some failed to find the group and were then lost to the network. Another coven met in a public venue that had two entrances. The phone signal was weak at the venue and on occasions members came to the venue and struggled to find the members. The lack of suitable venues, however, meant that this venue continued to be used despite the issues.

These types of problems are far more damaging than those running Wiccan networks tend to realise. Generally their organisation is based around a few close friends who know each other well and new people although important are nice to have rather than vital. The problem is that if groups are not vibrant and recruiting new people then gradually some of the existing members may lose interest. Momentum is vital when trying to gather together the thirteen people required to form a coven. Once there are thirteen it is likely to be self-sustaining however there is a limit to how long people will wait to be part of this. For this reason it is vital to make a very intense effort in the early stages of coven formation

A further problem relates to digital meetups. It can be very difficult to manage large numbers of people coming into a digital meetup. As a result it is very easy to fail to connect all of the members who wish to join. In order to avoid this it is important to open up the room for the meet up as early as possible. It is also important to tell everybody that there will be no late arrivals. The reason for this is that if people are clear that they will not be allowed in if they come late then if that becomes the reality then they will not feel agreed and they will blame themselves. If, however, people arrive early and can't get access because the organiser hasn't set up the event they will feel that the organisation is poor and will not return.

Of course it is preferable to try to catch all the potential attendees and to set up the meeting in such a way that there is a chance to catch those who are five minutes late. Members who pay no attention to the time of the meeting, however, will be more of a problem than a benefit. It is important to penalise those people so that they don't continue to arrive late for talks that are planned.

One of the ways to do this is to keep late arrivals waiting until an interval, but this must only be done if they have been clearly told that late arrivals will not be admitted at all. In this case they will not feel that they have been treated harshly. The same principle applies where a rite is being run. Those who arrive late can be told they are welcome to join after the rite has taken place but they cannot disturb the rite in progress. As long as they are told this in advance if they are unlikely to feel aggrieved.

A further problem that arises is the timing of events. It is easy to put an incorrect time, the wrong year, p.m. for a.m., Saturday for Sunday, dates and days that don't match and many other minor issues of this type. It is really important to avoid this. In one coven the leader of the coven was in the habit of arriving late for their own events, often up to 30 minutes behind schedule. Another member would 'hold the fort' but the overall impression given was very poor. All of these problems must be considered before even establishing the first event.

In summary the organisation that is being established needs to be professional in that it responds to organise people well but doesn't give too much slack to those who weaken the structure that is created. It is this approach that is the strongest draw for people joining the network and will ensure that the network remains strong.

9. Getting connected and preparing to form a coven

The first stage in establishing a coven is to gather a group of people who will form that structure. For some this is simple since one of the primary motivations for forming a coven is often that a group of Wiccans, or witches, wishes to practise together. Where an individual or solitary Wiccan wishes to form a coven, or where a couple wish to form one, there will be a need to find members. This may also be an issue for larger groups who wish to build a full coven. This means that understanding how to find members is a key issue for those looking to establish a coven.

The first stage is to connect with the Wiccan community to see if there are others who are interested in establishing a coven. How you do this depends on where the people who are interested in Wicca gather in your area. If there is a local Witchcraft shop you may be able to tie up with them. Alternatively you can use Meetup or other digital media. Meetup is a good option because it is local, however Facebook is also possible.

It is possible to simply establish a group on Meetup or Facebook and invite members to come to a meeting in a pub or coffee shop. This may be effective however often it is difficult to get a group up and running solely using this approach. This is, however, the starting point. In both of these cases it will take time, typically six months to a year for people to find you and connect with the group, or for you to connect others who you meet to your group, however if you persevere and maintain a public presence over an extended period it is likely that you will be able to connect with others locally.

The key issue when dealing with any kind of digital or print media is that quality matters. You need to produce high quality events and advertise them in an attractive way. If you don't do this you are unlikely to attract the best people, people will not invite their friends and progress will be slow. It may lead to a situation where you cannot understand why things are not working as you wished. If you have a quality driven approach from the beginning things will work far more effectively.

One of the keys to this is to view your group as a member would. This is done by having two accounts on Meetup. The first is an admin account and the second is a member account. This allows you to see what the members see.

A good approach is to establish a digital forum to co-ordinate the group prior to the first meeting. This can be done on Facebook, however in practice covens work better when there is a freer flow of information between the members and a higher level of equality in submitting comments to a group. This is a reflection of the egalitarian nature of Wiccans. For this reason the use of WhatsApp groups has proven to be an effective approach, although there are other similar forums which would be as appropriate.

Understanding the people who join

When joining people to the networks it is important to think about each individual member and what they are looking to get out of joining. It is important to ensure that they continue to get that. This is different for different people. Some will be looking to practice, some to learn, some to write rituals, others to socialise and others to be part of pushing the development of Wicca forward.

When it comes to arranging meetings people will have different reasons for attending and this will be reflected in the way that they approach coming to meetings and the reliability of their attendance.

Once you have members it is important that they are not lost so it may come to a stage where you need to invest time in ensuring that problems that individuals have are dealt with. This can be very draining, particularly where there are disagreements between people. This is because the disagreements often lead to people leaving the network and resolving them may be difficult

Running a Wiccan WhatsApp Group

The Watsapp group of a coven or pre-coven is a place where Wiccans can be connected to communicate. The main purposes are training, arranging meetings, running remote rites, noting key astronomical events and showing books or Wicca related items that are important to an individual. The forums also provide a place for general chat.

Joining a Watsapp group is very straightforward and doesn't inconvenience an individual significantly in the way that attending meetings does. For this reason a Watsapp group is a way to connect the key potential coven members prior to a face-to-face meeting. The members can be found through a Facebook or a Meetup group, personal contacts or through a range of other methods. It provides an easy way to regularly communicate with members.

Recruiting for the Whatsapp Group

The key to running a WhatsApp group is to ensure that you have a core of people communicating in the forum and that you add in new people regularly to create life. In order to get the forum to work you need to have a stream of members coming in. There are a number of ways to achieve this. One is to establish a website that offers to connect people in the area for Wicca training.

The method used to find members will vary. It can be a standard website, a Meetup Group, or a Facebook group. It can be connected to one of the existing networks of Wiccans that exist around the UK, or be independent. Once it is established it is important that the group has a purpose and is lively. This is the reason why training is so important since having a group to support training and to allow the asking of questions is a key function of the group which means that it has a purpose. If the group is too busy it is possible to establish a second route for the trainees however this will not stop the initial group from functioning as the trainees will leave messages in that group as well.

Once the group is established you need to have a system for bringing people in which ensures that they understand the rules of the group. The way to do this is to ensure that all members come into the group via a 'portico'. A portico is the entrance to a building that is attached to it but is outside the main door and this is the function of a portico to a WhatsApp group. In the case of the portico the function of it is to explain the way that the group functions when new members join. This allows them to have some idea of the purpose of the group, which achieves smooth running. Additionally this ensures that as people come into the group that they will be welcomed. This will make the group more interesting to those who are already members and give a positive impression to the members who join.

Controlling the group

In order to keep the group alive and functioning well it is possible to to put interesting information into it. This in itself is an art and it is best to post as much high quality information as possible.

This can include information about new books that have appeared that a Wiccan has purchased, astronomical events that are taking place, tarot cards that have been issued or which are owned. These should be put in a time when the group is quiet to make it clear that the group is still running and training courses accessible.

It is very important to avoid arguments in the group. The way this is achieved is by monitoring it. Until the coven has thirteen members the Magister or Maiden building the coven will need to monitor it. If they do not there is a real risk that arguments will develop in the group and destroy the work that has been done building the network

When people join the group it is important that they are given a good set of etiquette that allows the group to function well. In order to ensure that the group is a success it is important that it is, as far as possible, a friendly group. You should at all times avoid any kind of argument. The way to achieve that is to state that the group is for Wicca only and not for politics or general argument. If someone wishes to engage in this they can be offered a second group which is one where heated discussion and arguments are permitted and it will allow any post to be redirected to that. This can be done by cutting and pasting the comments if arguments develop. This keeps problems away from the main forum which needs to be protected.

The forum is important because it allows you to get some kind of idea of the type of people who are coming into the group prior to their membership. It will soon be evident which members have mental health issues or drug issues or who are generally argumentative. This allows a strategy to prevent those people from disrupting the training group which is at the heart of the coven that is being formed.

Making the group interesting

Since the covens form out of the Whatsapp groups it is vital that they are nurtured. The primary function of the Whatsapp group is to answer questions from members, however this alone is not enough. More life needs to be given to the group and this is done by posting interesting info. It can be challenging to think of new ideas, however there are common themes that can be used

Remote rituals

One of the best ways to provide a heartbeat to a group is to celebrate the full moons and the solstices, equinoxes and cross quarters. These can be celebrated with remote rites. This takes the form of lighting a candle providing a reading and everyone performing their own ritual at midnight or earlier. It is also good to get people to take a photo of the moon. The event should start at sunset in summer and in winter at 9.00 pm.

Training

The group can also be used to offer training. One of the best forms of training is plant/tree and crystal recognition. This takes the form of putting a photograph of a crystal, tree or plant and asking people to recognise it. In addition to being a fun thing to do it also provides knowledge and this is often what people who join Wiccan groups are looking for. When you have a set of crystals that are known you can create words that are made up of the first letter of each crystal.

Book Reviews

A further option is to post reviews of books that an individual has purchased. This is likely to be of interest and since most Wiccans have many books this is likely to be of interest to many people in a Wicca group. One way to do this is to have a weekly book slot which will provide variety. This is a task which can be given to an active member. This type of post is not needed indefinitely but is useful at the start when the group is initially forming.

Dealing with arguments

It is vital that arguments are prevented at all costs. It may be that arguments flare up before they are noticed, however sometimes they will be spotted whilst they are ongoing. It needs to be made clear in the group etiquette that in the case of an argument that members will be moved to a separate temporary Watsapp group. This can be termed 'The Chessboard'. Any member who has an argument with another member will be required to argue it out on the chessboard or be dismissed from the group. At this meeting it will be made clear to the arguing members that they must not destroy the group through an argument. The chessboard is an occult practice used to resolve arguments.

Using e-mails

Over time anyone running a group will acquire the email addresses of people interested in Wicca in their area. These will come from personal contact, from the website advertising your group and from many other sources. This e-mail address collection is easy to arrange through Weebly or other web systems.

These email addresses are very valuable because they allow you to quickly reach large numbers of people who are interested in Wicca. When you run events you need to have the maximum reach to tell people that an event is happening. A list of e-mails is a vital element within this as you can quickly contact those likely to be interested in an event and you are not dependent on paying a third party. This means that managing email lists is a really important skill as is creating attractive emails. For this reason when building a coven you should try to get emails of members and use them intelligently to contact people.

Organising a public meeting for an initial ritual group

Organising public meetings is important when building and growing a coven. Once the coven leader has established themselves as a member of the local pagan community, and set up a WhatsApp group to coordinate their contacts the next stage is to establish a public meeting. This would be typically a social event getting together people who already know each other online.

This event can be held in a pub, a library, a park or a coffee shop. Each of these venues have their own distinct advantages and disadvantages and it is worth trying different options. The most commonly used venues are the upstairs rooms that are available in some pubs. If the event is held on Tuesday or Wednesday night many pubs are relatively empty and will allow the private use of a room if there are likely to be a reasonable number of attendees. This allows a quiet space to be made available. The best location will be dependent on the particular town or city in which the event is held. The purpose of this event is to get to know the members and to establish who in the group will be interested in being involved in the formation of the coven.

The formation of a coven takes place in two stages. The first stage is the establishment of the initial seven members who will form the base of the coven. The second stage is to bring in members who will make up the coven membership.

If a coven is formed from scratch without a strong base of at least four members it can be fragile and may be difficult to maintain. If on the other hand there is a strong group of seven members running the coven there will generally soon be others who will wish to join and it will be relatively straightforward to run and build the coven.

These initial four members are termed the watchtowers and it is helpful to allocate particular roles to individuals. The roles are termed the watchtowers of the north, south, east and west and reflect the elements of earth, air, fire and water.

The Watchtower of Fire is the voice of the group and this is typically the watchtower that recites the drawing down of the moon if the Maiden or Magister does not do so. The Watchtower of the North, or air, should be taken by someone who is dedicated to supporting the coven. This is because they will be at the right hand of the Magister or Maiden of the coven and they will depend on them in the rite. The Watchtower of Water is taken by someone who is able in performing ritual practice including sweeping the circle and casting the water. The Watchtower of Earth would be typically responsible for taking on the role of the

Summoner if that person is not available and has an important role in helping to coordinate the coven.

If there are more than four strong individuals at the beginning then it is possible to split the role of summoner from the role of Earth and also to split the role of Fire from the role of leading the Coven. The key to determining whether there are enough people is simply attendance. if in order for the coven to run well it is vital that the members attend and as a result the spaces should be allocated only where there is certainty that an individual will attend.

Initially it is not necessary for the coven to meet monthly. It could meet quarterly, for example. The key, however, is that those who say that they will be part of the coven do make firm commitments which they meet regarding attendance. The agreement should be between coven members to run for a year. At the end of this period the situation can be reviewed.

Whereas the watchtowers need to attend, members do not need to make such a firm commitment. They will come to the coven later as they are trained and since this training is likely to take a year there will be an extended period for the members to join the coven itself.

The purpose of the social events is to find these members so that the coven can be established. Once the cover is formed it will create a strong draw for others looking to join and is likely to sustain social events. As a result it is important to find good people to take these roles. A good member is not one who attends infrequently but someone who can guarantee attendance in advance and keeps to their commitment.

What to do at the initial public event

For the very first event it is possible to have a pure social gathering where members chat, however after the first event it is important that there are talks, speakers or other types of training. Groups that simply consist of people chatting will generally dissolve after a few meetings whereas if good speakers are brought to the event it is likely that they will continue indefinitely and provide a strong basis for establishing the group.

This is the end of the first stage in establishing a coven. At this point the organiser of the group will have become known as a member of the local pagan community. They will have prepared their lineage, training and tools and have a working digital group on WhatsApp. The next action is to have a public meetup, to which people will come to because they know you.

Once the coven organiser has connected with the community and has a digital group, they organise a public meeting and then ultimately run a rite if there are enough people to do so. This rite is in public and is typically for the solstice, equinox or cross quarter. The next action is to run a private rite at the full moon or on the festivals of the Wheel of the Year for a small group. That is the way that the coven will develop. If a set of members have proven regular attendance which is driven by magic and a desire to meet others then ultimately this group is likely to become a practising coven.

10. Finding a magical site and running your first rite

The preparation for forming a coven can take many months, however ultimately it will be completed and it will be necessary to run the first rite. In many ways this is the key point for any coven being formed. Everything else up to this point is preparation, but from the moment you establish a ritual practice in some sense the formation of a coven is a natural outcome. Without public access ritual practice a coven will not generally form, but with it the formation of one is to some extent inevitable.

Given the importance of the establishment of ritual practice it is vital that the arrangements for the initial ritual are fully planned and that everything is done to ensure that the event runs well.

A large part of this is the preparatory meetings which are held in public for those who are interested in being part of a Wiccan or Witchcraft practice but do not have rites associated with them. It is not advisable to try to establish ritual practice before a couple of effective meetings have been held on an informal basis to connect those who are interested. Prior to the point of the first ritual the group will have met in person and this allows the Maiden or Magister of the coven to assess whether there is sufficient interest to establish a ritual practice which gives a good chance of the ritual running well.

Naming the Coven
One of the most powerful aspects of forming a coven is to provide it with a name. Names of covens are very important in establishing their credibility and it is important

to have a good and meaningful one, rather than one that is frivolous. Even having a frivolous name on a temporary basis is a problem because it may become attached to the coven.

It is possible to put off the naming of a coven but many of those who lead covens will have a name. Even if there is no obvious name for the coven, however, the point at which the first ritual is run is a good time to introduce a name for the coven, even if it needs to be changed later.

The name of the coven will often be determined by the lineage which it derives from. Those covens that derived from the horse traditions will often have a word related to the horse in their coven name. Some coven names will actively reference the name of the coven that trained them in their practice.

It is important to avoid naming a coven on a haphazard basis without thought or to pick a name that doesn't imply that the coven is serious. As much history and meaning as possible should be placed into the name.

The coven may also have a logo or symbol that it is associated with. This can become important later when it may be placed onto jewellery which a coven may use. The logo is often connected to some extent with the name of the coven and as a result consideration of the logo should be given at the time that the coven is named.

Finding your site

The initial stage in organising the first ritual is to find a site which can be used. There are three main considerations when considering the use of a location. The first of these is the magical nature of the site itself, the second is the privacy of the site and the third is the accessibility of the site. These three need to be balanced against each other as no location will be perfect.

The first consideration is the magical nature of the site itself. Some sites have a magical feel. This is due to them being private, having an enclosed nature or their being by the side of water or on the top of hills.

A good site for ritual practice could be a beach as this provides a good sightline for the sunset and for the planets. A second option would be a stone circle or other ancient site close to the area where the coven is being established. A third option is to use woodland.

One of the problems with this however is that many of these sites are not easily accessible for those looking to attend. It is possible to drive to a ritual site and this is a good option if you have two vehicles, however if only one vehicle is available it can cause an issue where it is impossible to get everybody to the rite.

One of the main problems that can occur if there are only two vehicles is that one of them has a problem on the day. As a result it may not be possible to perform the ritual with everybody who has agreed to take part. For this reason it is preferable in the first instance to establish the meeting point at a place for which it is possible to walk to the spot where the right will take place.

Unless the failure of all car members to attend would not prevent the rite from happening you should not organise a rite that requires vehicles unless there is a secondary location within walking distance of the meeting venue. The normal number of attendees at an initial rite could be six so as long as two of the others have cars then if they do not attend then before remaining will be able to go by car. But if there are six members and only two of them have a car then the failure of the person to attend who has a vehicle will mean that one person cannot attend the rite and this is very damaging to the atmosphere because all of those attending will be concerned that they are going to be the one that is excluded.

It is important that a proper check on the available sites takes place and that the Magister, Maiden or HP/HPs establishing the coven has a range of options available to them which will allow them to select a site which is feasible for the ritual.

The third issue that needs to be considered is privacy. Often the first rite will need to take place in an area which is close to a pub and as a result may have people walking through it. It is extremely difficult to find sites where this isn't possible particularly in the case of dog walkers. Dealing with dogs/dog walkers at rites is something which is important to be prepared for as it is the most likely form of interruptions that will be seen.

Additionally it is best not to use a site that is currently used by another group since the event may need to be advertised in public and as a result the other group may intervene and prevent its use. It is therefore important to find your own area and not to publicise the exact location, to the public. The location of the site can be passed over verbally to members or within a WhatsApp group that only has those who are attending the rite in it.

In order to get a feel for the types of location that may be useful it is helpful to visit some of the main sites that have been used for ritual practice by Wiccans historically. An example of this is the Thirteen Oaks in Highgate Wood which has been a site of ritual practice since the mid 1960s. This is a good example of a woodland location. Another important site is the Stiperstones in Shropshire which is an example of a hill based site. In the case of the use of beaches there is less differentiation between different types of examples and many have been used. Botany Bay in East Kent off season when the tide is out is an example of the type of beach that is a good ritual site.

It is not necessary and maybe unhelpful to use paid venues. The reason for this is that it creates an additional complication in terms of charging members to attend the ritual. Some groups do charge for attendance however it creates a different type of coven which is more akin to a public practice rather than a coven which operates as a group of friends. It is probably better to establish a functioning coven prior to hiring rooms or charging for attending rituals and whether charging is ever beneficial needs to be carefully considered.

No site is ever completely perfect and as a result a compromise will inevitably be necessary. But at some point a few weeks prior to the rite taking place it is necessary to decide on the location and start to consider how it will be used in the performance of the rite itself.

Planning the rite

The rite performed should, if possible, be a coven binding rite for the Maiden/Magister and the four quarters. If there are more interested in roles then the position of Summoner can be allocated as can additional positions but in general it is not necessary to have more than seven roles. If there are more than seven members it may be better to delay allocating all of the roles until the dedication of the members has been assessed.

When formalising the rite you should incorporate as many ritual elements as possible. This may include crossing a river to get into the ritual space, the giving of a coin for the ferryman, the use of a stang and other related elements. It is also important to have a sense of drama when performing the rite.

Once the Magister or Maiden who is planning the rite has selected the site they should look at it in detail to see how the ritual environment can be used to inform the rite itself. This approach is particularly associated with the Cochranian Tradition. This is because Ron White used Queens Wood as a ritual space. Part of that was that there were two small brooks that ran along the ritual site and these we used to create an island feel to the main site which is closely aligned to the view of the magic circle in the Cochranian tradition.

There are many different approaches that can be used for example if there is a lake or pond the positioning of the ritual in relation to that water will be important. Additionally if there are good sightlines to the horizon in particular directions then the position of the setting sun and the appearance of the stars and planets can be considered. It is particularly important to consider the position of Venus, which is the brightest of the planets. It will always be noticeable in any rite after sunset if it is in a clear sky.

The key to a successful rite is that it has a purpose and that the Magister or Maiden has a good sense of drama and the ability to create a magical feel within the rite itself. This is often dependent on thorough preparation.

The first consideration when planning the first rite is to determine whether a lunar or solar cycle will be used. There is no absolute answer to this. In the long run the use of the lunar cycle is important in coven practice because it allows for a more regular and structured operation of the coven. In the early stage, however, the members will be familiar with the Wheel of the Year and the importance of a particular solar sabbats, such as Mayday, Imbolc, Lammas or Halloween. As a result it is generally better to establish the first rituals on a solar cycle basis so that the particular elements of that cycle can be used. If the cross quarters are used this also allows for the second ritual to be established at the next cross quarter.

It may be that the rite does not completely succeed or completely fail and that there are dedicated attendees but not sufficient numbers to allow for the formation of a regular lunar cycle practice. In this case it becomes simpler to run the next rite as part of a series if the first one has been run on a cross quarter.

Within the rite itself then it is important to be clear about the practices that can take place. The primary issue is that the basic structure of the rite must have been created. This will involve the calling of the quarters, the sweeping of the circle, the sanctification with salt and water and the Drawing Down of the Moon. This acts as a container, within which the rite itself is held. The primary events within the rite depending on the time of year are as follows

Imbolc: This festival is the celebration of the goddess Brigid. The primary action is to take a corn doll of Brigid to the circle. Within some traditional practices there is also a corresponding male figure called the Holly Boy and it is possible to bring these two to the ritual with the corn doll termed the Ivy Girl. The form of the ritual traditionally practised is the burning of the corn doll however this is difficult in some public locations. It is, alternatively, possible to burn some corn prior to the ritual and to place it in the ground during the ritual to symbolically connect the corn from the previous year to the planting in the current year.

May Day: The primary celebration of May Day involves the Green Man. The celebration is of the coming of new life. It is also the time of the Milk Moon and this is celebrated by the giving of milk to Robin Goodfellow. One aspect of ritual practice that can be used is to pour milk into a bowl and to to read from a text that relates to Robin Goodfellow.

Lammas: Lammas is the loaf mass and is the time when the first loaf is created. This can be celebrated with a particularly attractive looking loaf. It is also the time when John Barleycorn is celebrated. He is a figure that is made from the first cut of corn. There are a number of traditions which are associated with John Barleycorn including a well-known folk song and this can be read at the ritual.

Halloween: Halloween is the most significant of the cross quarter festivals and is celebrated with a pumpkin. It is a time of visiting the other world and as a result the use of the poem the Preiddeu Annwn. This is helpful as it visualises the trip of Arthur to the other world.

What is actually done within the rite itself is dependent on how well developed the coven is. If the coven has four quarters allocated to it then it can proceed to the next stage. This is the binding of the coven. In this ritual the four elements hold a ribbon, as does the Maiden or Magister, and these are connected to the stang. It is then turned binding all the ribbons to the stang and the ribbon is then tied at the bottom. The ribbons should then stay on the stang until the time that the coven is formally created or until those members who agreed to form the coven are no longer part of its development. In the latter case the tibbons are removed and new elemental watchtower guardians will need to be found.

This ritual cannot be run repeatedly so it is important to ensure that before running it but it is clear that those who are taking part in it are committed and dedicated to the practice. But in general this binding ritual has been effective in making it clear to those members who take part in it that they are committed to the creation of a formal coven. Those who take responsibility for an elemental quarter should, if possible, not be removed other than at Halloween when all positions in a coven and membership of the coven itself is determined.

Sometimes there are a large number of people who want to be part of a coven and in this case there may be more than enough to cover the Watchtower Guardians. In order to resolve this problem additional roles can be allocated. These roles are those of the Summoner, the Magister and the Maiden. These three positions bring the coven up to seven, and any coven with seven dedicated members is ready to move into the next stage of formal lunar cycle practice or an eight event solar cycle. It is best not to bring more than seven people to the initial rite if it is going to be a coven forming rite. Instead it is best to form the coven at that point with the seven members and run a later rite which additional people are drawn to.

As far as the ideal time to perform the rite is concerned the most magical time is sunset, however if the site is difficult to to return from it may be a problem if the rite ends when it is dark. It is preferable that the rite ends in the dark, however in some cases the ritual space does not allow for this. This depends in part on the familiarity of the ritual site to the Maiden, Magister or HP/HPs leading the ritual.

It is worth becoming extremely familiar with the site so that the rite can take place at sunset. If this is not viable then the ritual should take place in the afternoon. It may also not be possible to run a ritual at sunset if it is taking place at the summer solstice however at the cross quarters it is generally possible to run the ritual at sunset.

The key to ritual practice is that it is magical and creates a sense of drama. A woodland ritual in a beautiful spot, or a circle cast by the sea, is by definition a magical and liminal experience, so it is beneficial to fully plan this rite. All elements of the right, however, need to be considered. This includes the robes and tools used in the ritual itself.

The most important thing when establishing these events is to not adopt a haphazard approach of simply putting the event onto Facebook and running a ritual as this is unlikely to be effective. Although establishing a coven is certainly feasible it is not an easy thing to do and a structured approach is likely to be necessary, particularly if a strong coven is to be built.

Assembling your tools and robes

One of the most powerful tools in terms of creating a magical ritual is the use of robes. There is considerable debate around whether a magician should make their own robes or whether they should purchase them. The best thing to do is to initially purchase a set, in order to get the coven established. The coven organiser can then look at the option of making them later when the coven is more established.

The best robes have hoods and are black with a coloured lining. The reason for this is that they create a unified feel for all of the members and create a sense of drama in the ritual itself. It is important to avoid a mismatch of robes as this will make the coven appear to not be serious and thus may struggle to attract members.

As far as the other elements are concerned it is important that you have all the elements in place prior to the start of the ritual. The tools are different between different traditions however generally a stang is required which is used to knock against the trunk of a tree before the members are called to the circle. Additionally a bowl is required to mix salt and water to cast around the edge of the circle and also another for the chalice.

There are two different approaches that are used with regards to these items and also with regards to the blade which is sometimes used. One approach says that these items should be indistinguishable from any items in a common home. The other says that highly ornate tools should be used. This is generally determined by the type of practice. If it is a traditional form of practice then the tools from the home are more common, whereas if it is a ceremonial magic based practice it will typically be the case that high quality items will be used. What is important is that there is a consistent approach and that the Maiden or Magister running the ritual understands the functions of the various items. They will need to be able to explain why a particular style has been chosen and explain this to the members of the group if required.

Announcing and Publicising the rite

Once everything is prepared it is possible to advertise the rite. Because there will already have been many arrangements made and a WhatsApp group formed simply advertising the event in the WhatsApp group should generate the members required to effectively run the ritual.

It is important however that other people are brought into the network and the first rite may represent a good opportunity to do that. For this reason it is a good idea to advertise the event on a Meetup group, Facebook group or any other social media. The description should state that it is a ritual group and that it is looking to establish a coven in the area. It should also state that those attending will need to be part of the relevant WhatsApp group in order to attend the ritual.

When you receive the request to join if they are known and you wish to invite them to the event then that should be done. If, however, they are unknown they should be told that they can come to the pre-rite drink but not the event itself. If complete strangers are added to the rite then it isn't feasible for that ritual to incorporate any aspect which represents the creation of a coven which involves them. For this reason it is best to ensure that there are enough people registered for the event to form a coven prior to those who have come through the advertising on social media being added to the rite itself.

The effect of this preparation is that on the day of the rite the situation will be relatively clear and that a group will gather who are interested in forming a coven, if there are enough. In general if there are five or six interested a pre-coven ritual group can be formed. Those who have come to the pre-rite drink will become the outer circle and will later be invited to join the coven if they are suitable. The inner core will practice together and should ultimately form a coven when the situation is stable. If there are insufficient members then a more open form of rite can be run and anyone could be invited, but this would not form part of the process of forming a coven.

On the day

On the day it is important to ensure that everything is prepared and for that reason it is vital to get to the ritual site as early as possible to check that there is no issue with it. From there the coven's organiser should go to the pub to meet the members.

The WhatsApp group itself will provide an indication of who is likely to attend and in general most people who say on a WhatsApp group they will attend a ritual will do so or alert the organiser of the event that they are not attending. Once the event is running it is essential to continue. In the worst case scenario where there are only two attendees a meditation could take place.

When the members arrive it is important to be friendly and relaxed and to greet them. One thing that can be useful to facilitate conversation is having a number of books that are related to the tradition that is being practised and discussing them. Alternatively having tarot decks available may be interesting for members.

It is also vital to have a narrative about the event about how the coven is going to practice and what it is going to be called. This will feed into the types of tools used and build an expectation that the ritual is going to be well organised.

It is important to state the leaving time from the pub for the ritual. If, for example, the rite has to take place at five o'clock to align with sunset then a good time to meet is at half past three. It should be stated that the group will leave at 4.30 p.m. There may be some slack but certainly by 4.45 p.m. it is best to leave and head for the ritual space. Sometimes members will arrive very late so it is important to not allow later attenders to interrupt the ritual in the middle. For that reason it shouldn't be absolutely clear where the rite is taking place except to those who are already at the event. If someone is extremely late they can be told that they will be met after the ritual.

At the first ritual it is not a good idea to ask anyone else to anything in the ritual or bring any item. The event should be run by the Maiden or Magister, but it should be made clear that later other people will be encouraged to take part and call quarters. It's not a good idea to try and train people whilst running the very first rite.

When you get to the ritual site you should follow the defined order of practice with as little improvisation as possible. Normally for the very first rite the Magister or Maiden will practise extensively and may even have travelled to the site a week before to perform a dry run. The key is to perform the ritual smoothly and for it to be as dramatic and interesting as possible and moving as possible. This will show the members at the Magister or Maiden is very serious and will continue to push ahead with building the coven over the months that follow.

There are a number of problems that can occur at rituals. One of them is that it can rain on the day. If this is the case then the time of the ritual should be moved slightly so that there is no heavy rain taking place at the time of the ritual. People should be offered the chance to not take part in the ritual. The ritual should not however be cancelled and it may be helpful to have an umbrella or two to ensure that those who particularly suffer from the rain have some shelter. There have been cases where there was torrential rain at events and in the worst case the rain continued for thirty minutes at a very intense level. Eventually the group walked to the ritual site and the rain eventually eased up.

An additional problem which all covens face is that dogs will come to the circle and take the bread. The best way to deal with this is to break the bread before the rite and keep half of it separate. Rather than battling with the dog, simply let it take the half which is in the open and then do not put the second part of the bread out, instead keep it away in a bag and put it out when the ritual requires it.

Generally at rituals things go more less according to plan and a moving like can be performed. Since running a rite of this type is quite complex it is possible that many of the attendees will not have experienced such an organised and structured one previously. Of course some would have been members of other groups but these groups might be unrobed without the option of being part of a coven. So it is generally a very different structure and given the unique nature of the event, with a deep meaning held within it, it should be possible for the ritual to take place and start to bring together the group which will ultimately become a coven.

After the event it is best to return to the pub for grounding and chat and then ultimately the members will return home. It will then be possible to determine the next event repeating the basic principle of the first one but continue to build the coven and the outer court.

11. Building to the Formal Initiation of the Coven and its members

The formation of a coven passes through a series of stages of which one of the most important is the first ritual. Once this is taken place the coven is in a far stronger position to move forward. Once this rite has occurred the focus of the coven needs to be on moving from being a loose group of individuals meeting in a pub to a functional and practising working Wiccan coven. This process takes place over a period of several months typically.

It is easier to begin by celebrating the solar sabbat, particularly the cross quarters which should be celebrated in all cases from the first ritual. However it should be made clear from the beginning that later rituals may take place on the full moon and the mark of an established functioning coven is a cycle of full moon practice. This is not to say that the solar cycle should be ignored, however these events should be for the more open aspects of the coven's practice where it is demonstrating its practice to the wider public who may be interested in joining.

In between the initial ritual and the formation of the coven there are likely to be three major considerations for the coven's organiser. The first aspect is the recruitment of members to the coven itself, the understanding of the types of members that are likely to join and how they work together.

The second aspect is the training of the covens members and events. This training does not need to wait until after the coven is formally established and should take place for any serious members. The initial training should not be formal and academic but take the form of one-off events. The first of these should be to teach the individuals involved how to take part in a ritual and the meaning of the elements of the ritual. A separate session on the background to the coven's formal practice may also be useful.

Where a group is part of a larger tradition it is possible that other members of that tradition may support the training. This may be done by offering access to their own online training or visiting the new pre-coven to help with the training of the members. It is likely for there to be the requirement to put together events, for example trips for the members of the pre-coven to start to build the links between the members.

The third aspect in the establishment of the coven is ensuring that everybody has the relevant equipment and understanding in order to form the coven formally. Friendship, magic and training are the drivers for the success of Wiccan groups and these must be nurtured at all times.

When the first rite has been run the members will often ask when the coven will be established. Generally those involved will want to form the coven as soon as possible, however this is not generally the best strategy. Whether a coven can be formed quickly or not depends on whether a group of previously trained and dedicated Wiccans exist within the group from which the members are to be found. If all of the people other than the organiser are new to coven Wicca then if it is established too quickly it is likely to collapse, normally after a few meetings.

In general therefore it is better to train all the members as much as possible before establishing the coven. Covens are generally fragile at first since the beginning is a delicate time in its life. It is, therefore. important that it is given the best chance of survival. This is achieved by ensuring that it has dedicated trainees in it.

This is counterintuitive, as those who are keen to see the coven established will press for it to be set up as quickly as possible, however those same members will often leave after a few meetings if they are not fully trained before it is established. Covens attract people who are simply curious. There is a tendency for them to attend one or two meetings and then leave.

Attendees of this type are extremely damaging to covens. This is because people will ask why so many attendees are joining and leaving. This is likely to be related to the type of person they are and not the actions of the current leaders. For this reason it is preferable to prevent these people from joining the coven in the first place and this is done by having an extended training program.

The fact that covens have experienced members joining and leaving means that there is a traditional practice within a witchcraft coven and this process is used to bring in new members. Generally a year and a day is long enough to ensure that an individual is serious about their commitment to Wiccan practice and this is the reason why this period is typically chosen for the cycle of initiating a new member.

Establishing a coven that is durable is far more difficult than many people expect. Setting up a coven which then collapses is very draining emotionally for the organiser and the members and therefore every attempt should be made to ensure the coven survives for at least twelve months after being established.

Holding back on the formal establishment of the coven ensures that it has the greatest possibility of succeeding. This doesn't mean that rituals cannot be run. They can even use the format that the coven will eventually use. The key difference will be that the members will not be initiated. This is because the initial dedications take place as part of the formal coven forming rite

There is an exception to the formation of covens slowly. This is where there are many members of the coven who are experienced practitioners who have been members of covens before, or who are absolutely certain to be dedicated. In particular if there are four people who have proven attendance over many months, or who have been members of covens before and have been regular attendees of them, then the extended wait before forming a coven can be bypassed. This is, however, unusual and unlikely to be the case. Additionally practitioners with such high levels of experience are less likely to be concerned about whether the coven is formed quickly or takes a few months. As a result even in this case unless there is an exceptional reason to form the coven quickly it is better to to allow things to settle for a few months prior to its formal initiation of the coven.

The key issue with running public rituals is that ad hoc attendees should work their way into it rather than immediately being an equal part of the group, calling the quarters and so on. If a rite is run then it must be run by either one person or four people. If it is run by one person there cannot be a calling of the quarters by members. The rite must be run for the attendees. Bringing in members to formal roles must be done carefully because if the wrong people are brought in at the beginning then it is very difficult to resolve that issue later.

Once the coven has been formed it is acceptable to run public rituals, however there must be a clear distinction between the Coven members and the general attendees. The coven member should be robed and there should be at least four of them if possible. This will mean that those attending these public rite will understand the formal structure of the coven and not feel that they can simply join and leave the coven without consideration of the impact this has on its formal structure. In this case the ritual becomes something that is done for the attendees by the pre-coven members. It is not necessary for the non members of the Coven who are simply attendees, often coming to the circle out of curiosity, to understand the deeper meaning of the ritual practice.

12. Events and training

Training provides an opportunity for an individual to learn in detail about the practice of Wicca. One of the problems that occurs is that members seek to get initiated without a proper location being found for the initiation. This happens because they are keen to get initiated and for them the location is not as important as the process of initiating itself. This a mistake, however, because the initiation cannot be repeated. If people are initiated in front rooms it won't provide them with a good experience to tell of their initiation later on and this will not encourage further people to get initiated. Being able to offer an initiation is a major strength of Wiccan covens and as a result they should be taken very seriously. Ideally they should take place in memorable locations, for example Dartmoor, Whitehorse Hill or particularly beautiful spots of woodland.

In the pre-coven stage training will consume a large amount of the time of the organiser of the coven. Since there will not be any coven meetings to deal with a very large proportion of the focus of the coven's leader will be on finding students and training them. This will ensure that the maximum amount of human resource is available to establish the coven when the time arrives.

The training course is likely to take the form of a set of events or lectures which run over a twelve month period. The students will therefore join the course and begin their studies. There are however a number of problems that can arise from this. The most significant problem that occurs is that the organiser of the coven does not fully prepare the entire training prior to the commencement of the course. They then become busy with the running of the coven and don't have time to prepare the training when it is required. This leads to a tremendous time pressure which makes running and organising the training unpleasant and undermines the motivation of the organiser. As a result it is therefore vital for the organiser to have the entire training arranged prior to the establishment of the coven so that the coven members can be trained without undue problems.

13. Recruiting members

As the coven organiser brings in members they will find that there are many different types of people who are drawn to Wicca. Some fall into the trap of saying that trainees are good or bad, however the key with them is not to judge them rather it is to treat them differently when they are different.

One of the key problems when dealing with members joining in the early stages is that the temptation is to take any member who seeks to be part of the coven. If potential members are rejected it simply leads to more delays and as a result it is tempting to take individuals who are clearly not fully interested in Wiccan practice or who have deep mental health or substance abuse issues.

Unfortunately taking in members of this type, whilst getting the coven running more quickly, will ultimately cause great strain in the coven in the long run. As a result it is important to consider very carefully when taking into the cover network any individual who had substance abuse issues or significant mental health problems.

Rather than taking them deeply into the coven in the first instance the best option is to seek an understanding of those looking to join and and hold off those members who look very difficult. It should not be necessary however to delay more than around one in ten potential members. Going beyond this will unnecessarily extend to coven formation period, however simply taking every member without any consideration of the long term issues is potentially a problem. Any individual with strong racist views will ultimately prevent members from joining the coven which will be an issue. They may also potentially create arguments with other members so it is important to avoid bringing into the coven members who have political views that will lead to other members not being able to join, or leaving.

It is not simply particular views that are an issue. It is also the way that the coven works together and the general ethos of the coven. One of the key problems faced is that covens can be either practitioners of dark magic or of white witchcraft. Mixing a small number of witches in a group where there are strong differences in regards to this is likely to lead to members leaving so it is important to be careful and consider how those joining the coven will get on with one another.

Dark Members: Dealing with Luciferians

The most common issues that occur relate to members with a passion for Luciferianism, Satanism or black magic. In most cases those joining will do so as a result of having been in other groups which have collapsed due to arguments or as a result of their inability to find a group as previous groups have failed. It seems that in practice there are almost no Satanic or Luciferian ritual groups that are able to sustain themselves.

The aggressive promotion of these types of ideas can be upsetting for those who seek a softer form of Wiccan practice that is based around the ideas of love and light. The most significant problem that is faced is from Luciferians promoting the idea that Lucifer is truthfully a spirit of the light and good. This is hard for people to accept.

Unfortunately those who are from a love and light school of practice will not accept this and become anxious that they are being inducted into a Luciferian coven. It is extremely difficult to balance these two positions however it is important from the start to explain that the practice which is to take place will not be challenging to anyone's ethics and that those who promote Luciferianism will be allowed to to join but that the coven itself will not be a Luciferian coven. If this is explained early enough then in the event of members interested in Luciferianism appearing then those who seek a love and light practice will generally not be put off.

Typically those who seek to practice Luciferianism are unable to form covens of Luciferians and this is why they join Wiccan groups. Those of a mainstream Wiccan view however have consistently shown that they are able to form groups relatively easily. As a result the best approach is to promote a mainstream form of Wicca and allow those interested in the darker practices to form their own subgroups if they are able. If a coven is allowed to become completely dark then it is likely that it will struggle to recruit members and dissolve in a few months. If there are a significant number of Luciferians, at least three in any case, then the way to deal with this is to create a group away from the main coven which acts as a safe space in which they can operate and which avoids conflict in the main coven.

Overly anxious members

A further problem that can occur is that there can be members who are unduly opposed to anything dark. Many are drawn to Wicca from the New Age community. They may join because they are curious, and leave if they find anything that concerns them. Where training is established then for the coven to survive or thrive it must be non challenging. However it is possible to inadvertently fall foul of the views of very sensitive individuals. One of the problems is that books may be promoted that have in them darker forms of practice and this may lead sensitive students to be concerned about where the practice is heading. As a result they may simply find a particular issue that they are unhappy with and leave.

The way to deal with this is to be clear continually that there will be nothing challenging in the practice and then seek to remove those aspects that are at issue. At first this may create a bland form of practice, however in the long run covens will split and all of those who continually object to particular forms of practice that are part of mainstream Wicca can be placed together at that point, thus resolving the problem.

Dealing with clear but aggressively promoted views.

Aggressively promoted views can be a problem in covens. Where students join who already have a very clear idea of what Witchcraft is they may want to impose this on the coven's practice. This can be reflected in a number of ways however the most common are the followers of Aleister Crowley, who published a large amount of material. Those who are drawn to Crowley will talk about this material and the ideas within it. Many of these ideas are objectionable to other people or are thought not to be Witchcraft. Crowley's links to Rosicrucianism, including the crucifix on his tarot deck, which are routinely owned by Crowley advocates, is a problem for some in mainstream groups.

Another issue is that those from a Luciferian perspective may push very difficult ideas. They may say, for example, that the swastika is truly a good symbol and should be used in rituals or that the upside down pentacle is a true symbol of Wicca and must be seen in rites. People with those ideas will sometimes aggressively push them and be prepared to argue points. This creates a bad atmosphere in rituals, and also in online groups, with the possibility of arguments breaking out.

A further issue relates to dual faith individuals. The main faiths that cause an issue are Buddhism and Christianity. Many Wiccans are hostile to Buddhism but also many are favourable to the practice. Buddhists will often promote Buddhist ideas causing arguments within groups. Those who continue to practise Christianity will also be met with bewilderment by many Wiccans who don't understand how Christianity and Wicca are compatible. Even those who are not truly Christian but are influenced by Christianity, for example promoting the use of psalms in rituals, will often meet tremendous hostility from people who do not wish to to practice rituals in which Christian elements exist. This is one of the most thorny problems that is faced within Wiccan groups. It is very difficult to shut down these types of arguments and yet very difficult to not aggravate those with these ideas.

The key strategy is the 'safe space' strategy which is that ideas that are challenging should be promoted in a separate area. This is generally a separate Whatsapp group, or one on one discussion with the group's organiser, and not in the general forums. This underpins all of the approaches related to this problem. You need to remember that the safe space includes the coven leader's involvement. Even in training these views should be separated and the proponent should be given a chance to discuss these ideas in a safe space for example a separate WhatsApp group.

The key to dealing with this is to not engage in discussion with people over these issues. These arguments cannot be won by either side. As a coven leader your role is not to push people away from what they believe but instead to provide clarity so that they are drawn to a group egregore or group mind. So the best way is to show polite interest, but not to go beyond that. It is vital that discussion about Buddhism or Christianity in particular is choked off as it is very likely to cause arguments if discussed.

The second way to deal with this is to split the groups and allow members to choose which group to go with. You must not allow the promotion of these ideas continually in forums where people cannot easily leave without damaging their membership of your group. The way that this is done is through 'leadership'. If you have a valuable member with strongly held views then you can provide them with a forum to promote them, for example a WhatsApp group, but don't get involved in that forum. You must provide a way out to those who don't want to leave a group but do not relish the arguments that may occur.

It is vital that as a coven leader you don't wear yourself out with endless arguments. If someone is dedicated to the use of psalms in rites then provide them with a chance to give a talk outside the group on this. Do not, however, engage in endless argument or allow that into the public domain. By providing a forum where these ideas can be discussed it makes it clear that there is no bias, but that the ideas should only be promoted to those who choose to listen to them. The success or failure of covens often relates to the coven leader's ability to avoid arguments and to calm them where they occur.

The problem of confused ideas

When you are building a group the most important thing is to avoid bitterness in arguments as this will cause people to leave. One of the main ways that this becomes an issue is that some individuals will promote confused ideas. These may be related to supposed or proven clandestine government action against the population, flat earth theories, health related issues or ideas about the occult which aren't easy for others to understand. If unchecked these are often promoted with great vigour and can cause many arguments within groups. These arguments are not related to Wiccan practice.

An example of this would be the promotion of the idea that the government is harming the environment with the use of chemical trails from planes. Regardless of whether there is any truth in this it has no bearing on Wicca, yet those who have 'understood' this often feel the need to explain it to others. The promotion of these ideas which are rarely of interest to anyone should be discouraged. Regrettably some of those will argue back and this should also be discouraged as it causes great problems and distress for both parties and severely damages groups.

The solution to this is to have a clear, well understood etiquette from the beginning. Once the problem arises it is too late because the person who has the confused idea which causes arguments will feel marginalised if their idea is suppressed. Only by dealing with this issue before it arises can the problem be headed off. The best way to deal with this is to have a written set of etiquette which is given to the members as early as possible after they arrive. The best place to put this is on a website that the members are asked to look at when they join. If this is breached the members should be redirected to that site.

This etiquette should contain a line to say

"In our groups, whilst we respect that some people hold views that the government and corporations are engaged in clandestine activities against the population there are also many members who do not hold these views. In order to ensure that the focus of the group remains on Wicca we request that members neither promote <u>or argue back against</u> these ideas in our online groups."

The main problem areas which have caused arguments are antivax, chemtrails, 9/11, the Illiuminati, the flat earth and Darwinism/anti-Darwinism. All of these have caused serious arguments in groups in the past and it is best not discuss them as this in a Wicca group if possible. If raised, however it is best to not argue against them and later raise the issue with a member if these ideas are promoted.

The coven leader needs to make it clear that it is acceptable to post these views on the members own social media, however this must allow people to disengage with their views if they wish to. It is important that members don't fall out with other members on their social media platforms. People should be told to simply unfriend anyone that they may be tempted to argue with. This type of guidance will head off problems without people feeling that they are being marginalised.

14. Building the coven's structure

One of the most important aspects of building a coven is to ensure that the structure of the coven which will maintain and sustain it going forward, in particular the roles of members, is clearly defined. Members need to take on those roles in the early stages.

A fundamental aspect is to allocate the roles of Guardians of the Watchtowers and the positions of Summoner, Magister and Maiden in the coven. The first task is to allocate the roles of the Guardians.

There is a practical basis for this which is that Watchtower Guardians call their quarters in the rite and someone therefore needs to be allocated to those roles. It is preferable that the same person calls these elements every single time. This will ensure that they are familiar with the element that they are calling and don't accidentally call a different element which can occur in rituals.

But beyond this there is a deeper significance for the allocation of the Guardians of the Watchtowers. Typically it will be the four Guardians that are the members that help the coven succeed. They are likely to have regular attendance at the coven's events. This resolves the problem for the Maid or Magister leading in the coven of whether there will be sufficient people to actually run the event. If the coven leader can be sure that there are four Watchtower Guardians then the event will run smoothly.

The Watchtower Guardians may also take responsibility for particular aspects. For example within Traditional Witchcraft covens the Magister or Maiden stands in the North and therefore whoever is standing in the North may be responsible for bringing and holding a Mullion Lantern. If they are tasked with it ensures that at all times there are at least two mullion lanterns in every ritual so that if a problem occurs with one there is a second one available.   *AIR*

A second role which can be allocated would be the responsibility for developing ritual practice. If there is a particular person who is interested in this then that should be allocated to them. It is not absolutely necessary to say that a particular position has a particular role, however it is best to have standards which can be loosely adhered to so this may be done by the Western Watchtower. This role may involve casting the ritual water and sweeping the circle.   *WATER*

The third position in a coven is that of Summoner. They are responsible for announcing and coordinating attendance at the rite. This is actually a very significant role. This entire role is about taking responsibility for the communications linking the Coven and and may initially be allocated to a Watchtower Guardian. They would, for example, take responsibility for allocating at the dates for the coven meetings on a Facebook group or Meetup site. This position could be held by Earth or the person in the Southern Watchtower since this role mainly involves activities outside the rite itself.   *EARTH*

FIRE [handwritten margin note]

The final role would be the role of Maiden or Magister to support the person leading the coven. This is a person who may read during the rituals and they will need to be confident in reading. There is no point in allocating the position of a support to the Maiden or Magister to someone who isn't able to read confidently so this person should take responsibility for reading poems in the rite including the drawing down of the moon. This could be allocated to the Eastern Watchtower of fire.

Broadly speaking this provides the three roles of Summoner, Magister/HP and Maiden/HPs to the South, West and East respectively and has one less onerous role for the North. This means that in the long run, when necessary, the rite can be run without the coven organiser.

The Coven Hierarchy

The name of the two key roles in the coven are generally the Maiden and the Magister. The word Maid can be used as a shortened form. The Lady of the Coven is a synonym for Coven Maiden. The word Maid is more commonly used where a working couple in a relationship outside the coven are leading the group. This is because the terms Maid and 'Mistress of the Profession', which is commonly used in Elizabethan texts, have acquired different meanings and as a result only established couples seeking a very direct connection with the older paths are likely to be comfortable with this. In situations where these relationships don't exist the term Maiden is more straightforward.

If there is a shortage of a particular gender the term First Maiden and Second Maiden should be used and First and Second Magister. In this case the title 'second' is used to take the role of the opposite title to their gender, so the Second Maiden acts as the Magister.

The third role in the coven of the Summoner can be male or female. These are the required positions of a coven, however if there are Watchtower Guardians these are not needed and the responsibilities may be taken by the Guardians.

Cords

Cords are used to show the initiatory level of the coven member. There are two cords in Cochranianism. The first of these is the white cord for a novice. The second is the red cord, which is for the initiate. If a member wants to use a cord and they are not an initiate they should use a hemp cord.

Within Old Horse Covens there is an agreement that the initiate will not form a new coven until a year and a day after they have been initiated. The black cord signifies that this time has passed. Typically this will be the end of their training and will be tied to a rite to celebrate that. These are purely traditions used in Old Horse Wiccan covens. This is not derived from the Regency and does not go back to Cochrane, however is a practical way to show that the member is able to establish a new coven in the practice. They should not do this other than at Halloween if they are involved in a coven which runs from Halloween to Halloween.

Other types of covens, for example those in the Gardnerian Tradition do not use cords. Establishing a working hierarchy is one of the most challenging issues in establishing a coven. This is in part dependent on the type of coven and the lineage from which it comes, but also is very dependent on the type of individual running the coven. Too tight a hierarchy can cause members to leave, however too loose a hierarchy can lead to the leader of the coven being insufficiently supported.

In some coven hierarchical systems the coven leader rules as an autocrat and establishes a strict hierarchy, which may be based on a hierarchy of initiates which is strictly enforced. This meets the needs of some types of Wiccans and should not be dismissed out of hand, but has many problems in reality.

These coven forms may require oaths of loyalty to the Coven Maiden, for example. In these forms of coven objections about the actions of the leader are not permitted and this may include skyclad practice at a particular rite. The member may then be forced to renounce their oath of loyalty and resign on the basis of a single aspect of coven practice. This can make this type of coven very brittle and subject to collapse. This type of approach is more commonly associated with those with Gardnerian initiatory lineages but can be durable, especially if the member's views are closely aligned.

In other structures the idea that 'all our peers' is normal and there is equality between all members. Individuals will be informed about the content of a particular rite and can choose to not attend if they wish without being forced to leave the coven. In this type of situation a Coven Maiden or Magister will typically avoid contentious approaches unless a member rather than themselves is running the rite. This type of egalitarian approach is closely associated with Cochranian Wicca.

There is no right or wrong in regards to this however when a structure is chosen the individual leading it must understand what they are looking to achieve and to apply that structure in an effective way.

Growing a coven is easier where there is a flatter structure however some elements of hierarchy will be required. The key is that, when the circle is created, the person leading a rite is allowed to run in their own way without interference. This creates a two-tier structure. The person at the centre of the coven determines who is allocated roles, but when those roles have been allocated the person responsible for them is in absolute control of the task, whether it is running a rite, running a WhatsApp group, writing a magazine or running a talk. There must be no interference once that person holds the coven stang or symbol of authority that has been determined to replace it in a given situation. This avoids the problem of members shouting out requests in the middle of a rite which can be disruptive.

This is not the case for the person running the coven overall. Although people to whom a task had been delegated, for example running a rite, have absolute power within that situation it is important that people can argue with the coven leader. Within this approach the coven leader becomes the point of argument not the person organising an event. If someone has a problem with the way that things have been run they must take it to the coven leader and not to the individual responsible for running the rite. They will then take it up with the person who's been tasked with the job.

If this isn't done and individuals are allowed to argue with organisers problems will occur. This is because there are a wide range of skill levels in interpersonal relationships. Some are skilled at diplomacy and others are quick to argue. A coven leader allocating tasks cannot be sure that at all times a task will have been allocated to an individual who is gifted in dealing with others. This will inevitably mean that on occasions arguments will ensue. These arguments would be very damaging to the structure and will create a situation where progress is constantly undermined by the breakdown of relationships.

If an individual has a very simple objection the coven leader can take it to the person running an event and modify it to deal with a problem. If however the problem is of a deeper nature the two members involved can be separated either into separate tasks. Alternatively if the coven itself and its ritual practice is an issue they can be separated into a second subsidiary coven on a temporary basis so that they stay within the overall group and continue to practice but not with the person who they don't have a good relationship with.

This might be seen as a severe punishment or expulsion from the coven however in practice this is not the case. Generally the person is very dissatisfied with working with a particular individual or perhaps because of a relationship breakdown and will be pleased to be in a circle without someone that they don't like, so the system works as a good safety valve.

The basic approach is as follows. At the centre of the group is a coven leader or a couple and around them are a group of members. The tasks are allocated to the members and when they have been allocated a task they take absolute responsibility for that task and their authority cannot be challenged. If people have an issue they can take it up with the person running the event but they cannot challenge the answer, whatever they need has to be accepted. If they have a problem with the answer they go to the coven leader who will either take up the problem or separate the two people involved. In an extreme situation they can remove responsibility for a particular task however this would be very rare.

One other issue is that people running covens will need to have an inner circle which is protected if the coven is to survive. This will be made up of people who have been fully trained and remain in the coven. One of the key approaches to getting a coven to work is to have a training cycle which sustains the interest of the trainee over an extended period which should be at least two years. At the end of this period space will be needed in the coven and and the members may be asked to leave the coven to establish their own coven or may proceed to a higher level course. If they are to stay beyond two years they will then enter the inner core of the coven the 'Sanctum Sanctorum' which is the ultimate core of the coven and is expected to survive over many years and ensure the long term durability of the coven.

This group is likely to be loyal to the coven leader. This means that they will operate as a group of friends and it is likely that they will in fact be close friends. At the very least they will have respectful relationships in order to support the coven. When someone is in the 'Sanctum sanctorum' they will have been trained for two years and be friends with the leader of the coven and they would not be able to be removed from that group easily. The only way that they would be likely to leave would be that they might temporarily give up their place in the coven if they cannot attend rites and become elders of the wider community around the coven, supporting its practice but not being part of its monthly activities.

This means that there is a structure within a coven no matter how flat it is. At the heart of this is the individual or couple leading the coven. Around them is the 'Sanctum Sanctorum' of fully trained members who have stayed in the coven. Then there are the initiated trainees. Then there are the uninitiated trainees, the novices.

The initiates are the red cords, those in the 'Sanctum Sanctorum' are the red, black and white braided cords. This cord structure is important so that everyone knows where they stand but this hierarchy does not change the basic structure of the organisation of an event. Even the lowest member cannot be challenged by a fully initiated three cord member if they symbolically hold the stang when completing a task.

Of course not all covens will use a cord system. There are many ways to run a coven. These types of cord systems are closely associated with Cochranianism and this might not be appropriate for an orthodox Gardnerian coven. Nonetheless all covens will face similar issues and will need to consider these issues.

15. Formally establishing the coven

There are many steps towards the establishment of a coven and these exist to ensure that the coven, once formed, is strong and stable. The most effective way to establish a coven is to proceed carefully, building the structure of the coven prior to its formation. If this does not happen some covens will succeed but there will be a far higher possibility of the coven breaking down in the period immediately after its formation. Where a group has been functioning as pre-coven with ritual practice for many months is unlikely that the coven, once formed, will run into serious issues.

Nonetheless there is a particular point at which the transfer from a pre-coven to a fully functioning coven needs to take place. The Maiden or Magister leading the coven will need to determine the date and form of the coven initiation rite.

The first thing to consider is the date that the rite takes place on and its location. These are significant factors because they will become part of the covens history and will provide memories which will sustain the group in the long term. For that reason it is important that thought is given to a coven formation rite.

The best solution is to form the right on one of the major festivals of the year, for example Halloween. Since there will typically not be time pressure on the exact date a wide range of possibilities will exist, however Halloween is associated with Witchcraft and is a good time to initiate a coven. There are however other options, for example

May Day or the Summer Solstice. If a coven has a particular reason to choose one of these then it can do so. Alternatively astronomically important dates are also used, for example eclipses or conjunctions. The key is that the date and location for the formation of the coven is part of the narrative of the coven's development and what the coven stands for. The creation of a coven on Halloween clearly ties the coven to Traditional Witchcraft practice so may be important for Cochranians.

The second consideration is the location of the initiation rite and this needs to be a location that is important to the coven. It could be the coven's ritual site but equally it could be somewhere that is used for reasons of privacy which are more important in the case of a coven formation rite than they are in general. Another consideration is considering the number of attendees since coven formations may involve bringing in members of other covens to support the new coven.

The coven formation ritual

Once the date and time of the coven formation ritual has been determined it is important to decide the content that will be used. The key elements of the coven formation ritual are firstly that the members of the coven who will be the first members are initiated or dedicated to the practice as novices. In the case of covens coming from the Cochranian tradition it is likely that all of the initial members of the coven will be giving the white cord of the novitiate at this rite if they have not already received it. This binds together all of the members of the coven.

Additionally at this rite it is important that the guardians of the watchtowers are fixed for the first year of the coven. They will typically have already been decided, however this initiation represents the chance to finally determine exactly who will bring the coven together and take over the guardianship of the watchtowers. These members will call the quarters at the coven initiation ritual.

The initiation of the coven should also include an acknowledgement of the stang with ribbons which will have been kept on the stan for that period. Following the ritual the ribbon should be removed from the stang and tied together in a single strand which can be used in later coven rites.

The exact form of the coven formation ritual depends on the tradition that is being followed, however if the ritual is part of a formal tradition then that tradition's practices will be used. If the coven is linked indirectly or directly to Traditional Witchcraft practices then this will be used to inform the coven initiation. It is vital that the Maiden or Magister controlling the rite are clear on the exact form of the ritual which will clearly involve many of the elements that are in a normal coven rite including the Drawing Down The Moon. It is also likely that wishes will be made for the coven's success.

Following the ritual is normal for the coven to eat together in the form of coven dinner. The more formal this is the better and it is important to clarify before the rite with the members what is planned. The venue, typically a pub or restaurant, should be booked. Alternatively since rituals for the formation of covens often take place in private houses for greater privacy the dinner may take the form of eating together at the property after the ritual has taken place.

Coven formation rites are rare and special events and will provide many memories for those who take part in them. As a result it is important that great care is taken to plan the event and ensure that everything runs smoothly. Sometimes gifts are given, which are items that could be used as part of the ritual practice, for example horse brasses, crystals, craft items made by a coven member or items specifically related to the coven. These gifts can be important in forming the culture of the covenant which is important in terms of binding it together.

16. The First Year of the Coven

Following the coven's formation it will move into its next phase which is to run its first year of ritual practice. This is tremendously important in the training of any witch or Wiccan since carrying out a full year of coven rituals will provide any Wiccan with a strong base of knowledge which can never be achieved from books. It will allow them to determine what happens to a whole year of practice and would typically make it feasible for them, if they wish, to run a coven of their own.

There are many aspects to coven practice. At the heart of it is generally the performance of the seasonal rituals. Prior to the establishment formerly of the it is necessary to determine how the coven will practise. The two basic forms are to use the Solar Sabbat cycle or the Lunar Sabbat cycle. In a fully formed coven the lunar cycle structure is often better, however some covens will prefer to use a solar cycle. It is not generally easy to use both a solar and a lunar cycle since the number of events is greater and these events clash making it difficult to plan for a coven. Nonetheless it is possible to do this if the solar sabbats are used for public events.

One of the key issues that will be faced when running a fully formed coven is that new members will need to be initiated into the coven and additionally the initial coven members will need to be given initiations themselves. This is important in the life of the coven since it provides events that need to be completed. Covens will also typically want to arrange trips to particular events. One of the main benefits of a coven is that it provides a group of people who are keen to go to the large Wiccan friendly events for example the Stonehenge Summer Solstice or the Butser Burning Man. It is important to attend these events since they will be attended together and this will make for a more rewarding coven experience.

There are many other types of events which have been part of the practice of covens. One example which many covens have done is a trip to Avebury. This is a free access site which is easy to use and which has a number of aspects to it which are able to create a one day activity. These include a visit to the West Kennet Long Barrow, The Sanctuary, Marlborough and to Silbury Hill. The circle itself is also very beautiful. There is also an excellent pub, the Red Lion, that many pagans are familiar with.

Another activity popular with Wiccans is a trip to Dartmoor. This is a site with long associations with Witchcraft and has the rare facility of allowing Wiccans to camp free of charge at the location. There are also many hotels and places to stay in the area and this allows groups of mixed campers and those staying in hotels to visit together. There are numerous sites around Dartmoor which can be used for rituals and it is a place that can be visited repeatedly.

A further option is visiting one of the large one day events run by some of the pagan networks. These take place around the country and generally include a series of talks about Wicca and Witchcraft. Typically a band also plays in the evening. There are also typically a number of stalls selling items of interest to Wiccans. These provide the focus for a day's activity for a Wiccan group and have provided some very memorable experiences.

Another option which works very well is to visit some of the folk festivals around the UK. These can be visited for a day as part of a camping trip. One of the best options is the Hastings Green Man festival which takes place in May. This is a quite straightforward location to visit and there are many events to take place at this site which link to the old traditions of Britain. The Broadstairs Festival is another option as is Stonehenge, which allows access overnight on the Summer Solstice. The Edinburgh Fire Festival which is held at Beltane, is another option. Music festivals are run on a continuous basis and watching for different festivals which are available in the local area is a good option. There are a number of festivals related to the horse traditions. The most prominent of these are the Abbots Bromley Horn Dance and the Padstow celebration. There are, however, dancing horses in many other areas for example Mari Lywd in South Wales and there are related traditions including the Haxey Hood in Lincolnshire. These are good options for a coven to visit if they are within easy driving distance.

For those involved in Cochranian practice it is important to visit the sites that are important within the Cochranian tradition, for example Burnham Beeches, the Stiperstones, Queens Wood, the Devil's Dyke and many others that will be familiar to those of the Cochrane tradition. For Gardnerians there are a different range of sites which are of historical importance to the Gardnerian tradition. Whichever tradition is followed this goes towards the creation of the culture of the coven and this will allow the coven to provide a rich experience for its members. It will also help to provide a good practice of Wicca for the first year after the coven has been formed.

17. Dealing with problems

One of the recurring features of Wiccan groups is conflict. Wicca tends to lead to the creation of strong relationships quickly but can also lead to friction. Understanding how to manage that is one of the biggest challenges to setting up a group.

The most important thing to understand is that arguments are very damaging for groups and the potential for arguments must be limited at all stages. One of the biggest problems comes from giving up power and responsibility to third parties. If that happens then arguments may develop between those who have been tasked with responsibilities and those who have not. It is best to hand over responsibilities slowly and with great care.

This can be a real problem. If, for example, a magazine is required, it is tempting to pass over the editorship to a third party. The problem with this is that arguments are very likely to break out between members of the editorial group. This may result in some of them leaving acrimoniously. It may be better to retain management of the project and hand out the work to individuals who are directly responsible to the coven Magister or Maiden.

It might seem that this would create more work, but in practice the problems resulting from arguments between members are often far more time consuming and damaging. It is best to control for things to be controlled by the coven organiser until they have a good understanding of the nature of the people involved. At that point it is less risky to pass over work to a group of members.

The two coven system

Despite the best efforts of any Coven Magister or Maiden, arguments are almost inevitable. When this happens it is helpful to have a two coven system to deal with problems. Initially there will be a single coven. As it grows small issues or disagreements will occur. Rather than struggling with this it is sometimes better that two separate but related covens are allowed to form. This avoids the need to formally expel people.

The second coven may not meet monthly. Instead it may meet infrequently, or quarterly. It will still be led by the Magister but will allow for the separation of people who have disagreements without forcing them to leave the coven structure altogether. At a later date members may be brought back into the main coven, or the second coven may break away as a whole.

Dealing with theological differences

One of the main problems that is faced in covens is how to deal with teachings that contradict the main teachings. The golden rule when dealing with these problems is to not shut down these theories or argue with them. Where possible they should be absorbed into the mythos and where not possible they should be allowed to stand as the theories of individuals that are tolerated in a broad church. The focus should be on making the core teaching and practice effective. Even if some members are not harmonised with the main group it is possible for them to coexist and play a valuable role in the coven. The focus must be on promoting and harmonising a clear set of ideas.

There are a number of possibilities for problems to occur but the issues falls into two categories. The first of these is that the students promote ideas that contradict scientific evidence. One of the main sources of this is the belief humans are descended from 'star people' and not a natural evolution from other life forms on earth. There are a number of other extra terrestrial ideas. This is easily dealt with where these can be absorbed into the mythos of Witchcraft without becoming a UFO spirituality.

Another issue is the promotion of ideas about the Golden Dawn, particularly related to the lesser banishing ritual of the pentagram, within Cochranian covens. It is common for members to want to perform the Lesser Banishing Ritual of the Pentagram. This ritual is beautiful and many find it effective, however it has a weak theoretical underpinning and the reason for the choice of the angelic directions held within it isn't clear.

When these rites are performed it is important to clarify the reasons for this and related rituals being performed. The fundamental reason is that the coven provides a stage for the performance of beautiful rites. This should be facilitated. However the symbolism behind these rites should not be included in the covens or they will prevent a clear and logical ritual practice from emerging. Within the Gardnerian tradition there is less of a focus on understanding the basis of rites and in any case it is aligned with Gardnerian practice so it does not cause conflict. On the other hand absorbing Cochranian practices into Gardnerian format covens may cause related issues.

A further problem relates to those who bring Christianity into covens. This is a significant issue as it may drive people away. In this case the key is to ensure that those who derive ideas from Christianity do not promote the ideas in the coven itself. A lot of the issues relate to the use of Christian iconography in their spells and magic but other issues relate to Wiccans attending church services and appearing to be primarily Christian. This may seem an unlikely issue for a coven to face, but it is far from unusual. In these cases separation of the two traditions is the best approach.

Whenever problems occur, however, it is important not to fight with people. In the case of Cochranian practice it is taught to a significant extent through riddles and people often want an easy answer, This has led to the creation of 'blinds' which are simple answers that carry no real meaning. In this case people just follow what they have been told without thinking if it is logical. An example of this is the Riddle of the Sphinx where a simple but meaningless answer was provided by Aeschylus but this does not provide a deep answer to the Sphinx's riddle.

What a coven leader must avoid is constantly undermining the members even if they are not being logical. It is better to just support people even if they do not have logical theories. Covens are supportive groups of friends rather than academic bodies and the building of a good atmosphere in the coven is an important objective. This atmosphere or energy can be damaged by arguments which don't really develop the coven even if resolved logically.

18. Keeping a coven running after the first year

At the end of the first year the coven will be reformed. This means that members can leave or form their own covens with no ill will felt. Adopting this approach stabilises covens and makes them able to deal with her far larger range of problems. Issues are inevitable within covens and some people will typically want to leave or form their own covens in the end. Many people will be able to put up with issues for a short period of time that they would not be able to put up with indefinitely and as a result having a natural breakpoint can strengthen the coven. So it is worth building this approach into the coven's practice and understanding the yearly cycle so that when problems do occur there are a range of ways to deal with them.

On other occasions, however, covens will be extremely stable for long periods of time. In order to avoid routine being an issue there are two main strategies that can be adopted. The first of these is taking new members into the coven and for those members, in time, to hive off in the coven to form their own covens. This creates a family of covens that can work together and allows for a diversity of members. These covens can also work together on a cross coven basis on projects that are of interest to the members of both covens.

The second approach is to use important astronomical events to inform the ritual of the coven and to make things memorable. These would include close conjunction of the planets as was seen in December 2020 when Saturn and Jupiter were conjoined. This also provided a very good chance to build a cyclical activity since these conjunctions occur occasionally and provide a memorable event which will not happen every year. In 1999 for example there were significant ritual activities around the total eclipse of the sun in Cornwall.

Another option is to write magazines, books or engage in other commercial activity together around the coven. This provides a method for engaging with the members over a longer period of time and providing a way for them to spend more time on coven activities. A common approach is for the coven to produce a magazine which is then sold to the general public. Alternatively the coven may run a festival to which other members of the public are added and this provides a focus for the activity during the year.

Life changes in the case of a coven's Magister or Maiden may mean that they may no longer be able to run the coven on the same basis. This can be the case if the person leading the coven leaves the area in which the coven is primarily based or if they become handfasted and have a family. This may make it difficult for them to run the coven.

Sometimes covens can be closed, however in general the links between the members are too strong and rather than the coven closing it changes from being a monthly cycle to meeting infrequently. It may be that the coven has created its own hived off covens that continue to meet and for those who want to continue to practise monthly they can shift to the new coven whilst retaining the connection to the old but less active coven.

Whatever happens it is important this takes place on a controlled basis as it will allow the coven to be reestablished as a regular practice if necessary. There are many covens around the country meeting occasionally to retain their member's connection with in person Wiccan ritual practice. These covens continue to perform an important role even though they do not meet with the same regularity as they met initially. There is a place for a wide range of coven forms in the Wiccan community.

Conclusion

Many people consider the idea of forming a coven to be arcane, romantic and possibly unfeasible. When faced with the reality of forming a coven it is clear that covens have always been part of our communities and probably always will be. For some being part of a coven is a burning necessity which never leaves them, for others it is a fleeting interest. But these disparate individuals can work together to create powerful ritual communities.

Covens provide a great deal of companionship pleasure and spiritual growth for those who take part in them. Those who have been part of a coven will generally state that it is or has been one of the most important spiritual events of their lives, and in many cases the first coven that they join will be the primary experience of their spiritual practice moulding their later development.

Given the importance of membership of Wiccan covens to those who take part in them, it is important that those running them make efforts to ensure that the practice is as rich and meaningful as possible. Wiccan covens fill a deep spiritual void within those who are drawn to Wiccan practice. For them often no other practice feels like home.

So those who take on the mantle of the Maiden or Magister of a coven had a deep responsibility to their members and to the community at large. They should be prepared to take this responsibility with great seriousness and to understand how to perform it in a way that is beneficial to the wider community. As with many other parts of life the return is largely determined by the efforts made.

It is worth reflecting on this at the start of the journey of coven formation since the personal relationships and the networks are of great value to those who make the effort to build these groups. Many coven leaders are deeply connected to and committed to their covens, and put their heart and soul into the group. It is these covens that ultimately have sustained the Wiccan and Witchcraft community over the generations and will continue to do so.

Index

Abbots Bromley	116	Golden Dawn	36
Alexandrian Wicca	29	Halloween	75
Book of Shadows	16	Haxey Hood	116
Buddhism	96	Hierarchies	102
Burnham Beeches	116	Imbolc	74
Chaos Magic	30	Instagram	46
Chessboard	62	Lammas	75
Circle	15	Lateness	51
Cochrane, Robert	13	Luciferians	92
Cochranian Wicca	30	Mari Lwyd	116
Cords	103	May Day	74
Correllian Wicca	33	Meetup	46
Coven dinner	112	Old Horse	37
Coven name	69	Pubs	63
Cross quarters	84	Public meeting	66
Crowley	95	Remote rituals	61
Crystals	61	Robes	41, 77
Cunning Man	34	Sabbat	15
Cunningham, Scot	9	Sanders, Alex	28
Dartmoor	115	Sites	67, 69
Dianic Wicca	34	Stang	112
Email	63	Stiperstones	17
Facebook	46	Summoner	100
Faery Wicca	35	Tools	77
Gardner, Gerald	12	Valiente, Doreen	27
Gardnerian Wicca	35	Watchtowers	64
Glastonbury	17	WhatsApp	56
Grimoire	43	Witch shops	53
Green Wicca	36		